HORSE RIDING

IN THE 21st CENTURY

DISCOVER THE ROUTE
TO YOUR SUCCESS

AVIS SENIOR

B.H.S.A.I

First published in 2015 by
Avis Senior Publishing
Email: avis.senior1@gmail.com
www.avissenior.com

This edition reprinted 2017

A CIP Catalogue of this book is available from
the British Library

ISBN: 978-0-9927665-4-2

Cover design and typeset in Bembo 11½ pt by
www.chandlerbookdesign.co.uk

Printed and distributed by
Createspace

CONTENTS

2. Anatomy enlightenment

The horse was not designed to be ridden! The author has concerns that riders and handlers of varying ability are not always au-fait with the location, operation, and possible detriment of the horse's anatomy. She offers a much-needed basic, yet informative insight into the temporomandibular joint, hyoid bone, atlas, the ribs in relation to the shoulder, nuchal and supraspinous ligaments and the latissimus dorsi muscle. The signs, effects, and simple checking procedures of the one sided horse are discussed, as are the damaging effects of feeding the horse from a hay net.

3. Evasion – Part 1: Our artillery

You will discover when probing into the reasons for the horse's evasion, that we are often the opponents as we lead our horses on an inadvertent path of destruction. We have the innate ability to transform our natural aids into built in artillery, all of which boost the influence of the other arms at our disposal. Sound practical advice opens up your mind to the simple options leading to harmony.

4. Evasion - Part 2: Our artillery

It is with the best intent that a rider places a saddle on the horse's back, regrettably often based on limited knowledge. The same rider often finds it hard to believe that the saddle and its array of accompaniments can actually be the cause of evasion by the horse, particularly when many of the evasions appear to manifest in front of the rider when in the saddle, rather than underneath her. Nevertheless, wherever the manifestation, the finger points at the horse. Here, the author, in her role as a riding coach, supportively describes and gives simple yet detailed problem solvers that will empower you to make informed choices based on the present fit of your saddle, and to seek help from an expert saddle fitter when appropriate.

5. The human anatomy

The significance of the human skeletal frame often appears to be of very little relevance when in the saddle, with emphasis placed on the muscles. The application of both, along with simple explanations of the differences in the male and the female skeleton, is described in chapter 5. An interesting addition is the modest clarification of the core muscles and other muscle groups used when riding. *If you walk from your knees, you will ride from your knees!* A light bulb moment for many. The short exercises described give realisation to the unnecessary waste of energy and effort you may exert on your anatomy as a horse rider.

A YOUNG COWBOY WAS WORKING SOME HORSES IN A ROUND CORRAL.
AN OLD COWBOY CAME BY, WATCHED FOR A WHILE AND THEN HE ASKED:

"YOUNG MAN, WOULD YOU LIKE TO KNOW
THE SECRET OF GOOD HORSEMANSHIP?"

THE COWBOY SAID HE WOULD. THE OLD MAN MADE A FIST AND HE SAID:

"IF YOU CAN OPEN MY FIST, YOU WILL LEARN
THE SECRET OF GOOD HORSEMANSHIP."

THE YOUNG MAN POKED, PRIED, THUMPED, PINCHED, SQUEEZED,
PUSHED AND SHOVED THE FIST.

HE FINALLY SAID:

"I CAN'T GET IT OPEN. WHAT'S THE SECRET OF GETTING YOUR FIST OPEN,
SO I CAN LEARN THE SECRET OF GOOD HORSEMANSHIP?"

THE OLD COWBOY SAID: "YOU COULD HAVE ASKED.... "

with the kind permission of Natural Horsemanship Saddles

Foreword

By Suzanne Rogers
Animal Welfare Consultant and Equine Behaviourist,
Learning About Animals

The array of available gadgets commonly described as 'tack' and 'aids' is a part of equestrian culture that is continually evolving and darkly fascinating. For a hobby and sport in which the people involved usually profess a love of horses, the fact that most of the equipment used is based on inventive ways to cause pain should be the cause of outrage and condemnation. However, the equestrian culture is such that it has become absolutely normal for tack rooms to be full of various bits, bridles, training aids, saddles, spurs, all professed to work through different actions. Although the invention of new 'aids' is evolving, that evolution seems to be towards items that would not seem out of place in the dark ages. As an equine behaviourist I am dismayed at the increasing number of options there are to control horses through pain and discomfort rather than consider the underlying causes for their behaviour.

Upon that cultural canvas Avis Senior has written this book with an honest agenda of walloping the horse owning community over the head with a solid no-nonsense account of the systematic abuse of horses. The book is written in a refreshingly honest way by someone who, as an experienced BHSAI, has authority in the field. Although the writing style is so far from the 'usual' it can be a little distracting, the non-apologetic manner with which the author continually and relentlessly urges the reader to examine how we are treating horses warrants respect, and more importantly, action.

As well as a plea for the reader to carefully consider the equipment they use 'on' their horse, the book contains very practical guidance. For example, the exploration of saddle fitting goes beyond the typical cursory look at fit and includes a wealth of useful tips to consider. The section on how human anatomy affects the rider is a crucial element that is often overlooked – after all it is easier to look to purchase a gadget then look at our own posture and skill.

I particularly like the way the author engages the reader in a way that feels so much more interactive than reading a book. For example, there are exercises that you can do from your armchair (or on the train if you aren't averse to some funny looks) and as a result when you put the book down it feels as if you have had one-to-one tuition with your own personal riding instructor.

I was going to say that this book is an important addition to the equestrian book shelf but I don't think it should be resigned to a book shelf, getting as dusty as the equestrian culture it explores. It should be passed on, read, pondered, discussed and be allowed to do its job of shaking things up pushing us into creating a new, more compassionate, equestrian culture.

By Ros Jones
Ros Jones BVSc MRCVS

■ There are no bad horses out there, none who are deliberately 'naughty'. What may be an undesirable behaviour to us (e.g. bucking, rearing, bolting), the human, is just a horse being a horse and acting instinctively in any given situation. It is therefore our responsibility to understand how a horse thinks and reacts in order to avoid these behaviours occurring. I feel that as a species kept primarily for leisure and sport, horses tolerate a great deal and are hugely misunderstood by humans who stick to their traditional views of equipment and training. In my experience too many people seem ready to use the latest bit of equipment or training tool (I would include some 'methods' in this category) to try and 'control' the horse, rather than taking the time to understand what caused the 'mis'behaviour in the first place and correct this underlying cause. As a vet I am aware of both the physical and emotional trauma that both rider and equipment can cause the horse and Horse Riding in the 21st Century certainly enlightens the reader to that fact.

It is time to start questioning how we train horses and with what tools, how we keep them and how we can have a relationship with them that is fulfilling to both parties. We need to stop just doing something or using that equipment because that is the way it has always been done. Although most horse owners would be mortified I am sure, to think they were abusive towards their horse, often it seems to me that they can't see it. I know I never felt happy using a flash noseband to stop my horse putting his tongue over the bit, but I did it because my instructor at the time told me I must. I didn't know better. Some years later (noseband and instructor discarded) I discovered bitless bridles and my horse sighed with relief. Our relationship and trust in each other improved hugely and it opened my eyes to just how much our horses put up with. For the open minded this book is an empowering and informative starting point on a journey towards a better relationship with their horse.

Author's note

This guide is a necessary read for all. It bears no relevance to how advanced you are in your riding or coaching career. However, it does resonate with the varying degrees of distress the horse may suffer at the hands of insensible handlers.

Trawling through the internet one day while taking a break from my manuscript, I came across a You Tube video 'Horse Revolution – The horse crucified and risen Part 2 – the effects of the bit' by Nevzorov Haute Ecole. It was shocking to watch. Nonetheless, it does echo the methods still used and passed down from those at the top of their discipline.

It also encompasses everything I had an overwhelming desire to include in what is a frank, but from the heart argument from the horses angle. You might want to watch the video prior to reading further. You may not realise that you may well submit your own horse to this type of abuse. Even actions of the kind disclosed in the video to a lesser degree are still abuse.

I generally refer to the horse as **he** or **she**, rather than **IT** and I will use the term he for ease of reference in this guide. The rider/handler, also for ease of reference (and for no other reason) regarding male and female, shall be referred to as she unless I refer to you as the reader of this guide.

The horse – a silent monarch

An introduction into how we believe we reign supreme over all species, will stop at nothing to ensure we stay at the top, and how we and our gadgets will stop the horse in his tracks if a struggle ensues through our attempts at domination.

The horse's plea:

I beg lay down your arms
Lead me; I will follow
Ask me; I will give
Protect me; I will be your loyal friend
Give me your heart; I will give you my soul
Understand me with mind, body, and spirit
We will be one

AVIS SENIOR 2013

The association between human and horse has evolved over thousands of years, from human predator v equine prey, to the human/equine relationship prevalent today. Friendship and trust are crucial in the survival of a herd.

The same are vital for human survival. However, our battle for supremacy within our own race is also prevalent.

We also believe we reign supreme over all other species and will stop at nothing to ensure we stay at the top. We try to dominate any being that happens to cross our paths; if a struggle ensues, our **artillery** will stop it in its tracks.

We humans constantly force our will on the horse without any consideration for his natural instinct and behaviour. We stole his natural habitat when we wanted it for ourselves; we then stole his freedom, with the expectation that the constraints we put on him would fit in with our ways and the restraints of our daily lives.

Much of the time, the horse is in a setting that is foreign to his species and his natural instincts, such as isolation in a stable. We don't pause to consider the loneliness he feels when we isolate him from his kind, despite his strong gregarious herd instinct. Despite all this, the horse tries his best to please us. He complies with our bid, usually with willingness but just as often with questions that are invariably ignored.

He desires and deserves strong but understanding leadership. However, much of the time we are more concerned with domination. We are the victors, we are the elite; we are ....HUMAN!

The horse lives in the moment and he has no feelings or emotions.

Do you really believe that statement to be true? The horse is instinctively aware of the moment for his survival, but his memory allows feelings and emotions to surface depending on the given situation he finds himself in, for example, the loss of a loved one, the joy he shows when he sees his friends, the panic he shows when faced with his nemesis.

Communicating with the horse

This piece sets the scene of the still existing common belief that horses and humans communicate only by body language, behaviour, and voice. The aim is to inspire you to read on with an open mind; to know that the horse tries to communicate his pain, discomfort, and lack of confidence to us daily, but his efforts are generally ignored.

There still exists the common belief that horses and humans communicate only by body language, behaviour, and voice. The horse does have a lengthy vocal vocabulary. He also has a rich sign language of which many equestrians falsely boast a strong understanding.

Regrettably, although he tries to communicate with us daily, we fail to hear him. This can be particularly distressing for him when his attempts at showing us the pain, discomfort, or lack of confidence he is suffering, fall on deaf ears. Rather than listening to his pleas, for example, an evasion of the bit when he is sore in the mouth, punishment is his reward for the evasion, in the belief he is merely naughty.

Kick it into next week; whip it; pull its back teeth out; drag it

are but a few of the phrases in earshot through the years.

Humans have labelled the horse unpredictable, but he is incredibly predictable: he licks and chews when he submits to our wishes, released of the stress he has suffered; his reaction and behaviour to our treatment of him is very predictable when we realise and accept that he is *not* human!

Generally, we know the horse has a sixth sense: he can sense changes in our mood; he knows when we are afraid or nervous. However, the sixth sense is only the tip of the iceberg.

Humans and horses can communicate on a much higher level than many think is possible - intuition, perception, clairvoyance, call it what you will.

There is no mystery in interspecies intuitive communication. It is simply a language of feelings rather than a language of words; it is the sending and receiving of thoughts, images and emotions, and being able to understand and interpret their meaning. I believe we all have the potential for it; we simply need to have the desire to exercise it.

This type of communication eliminates the need to read body language or make guesses as to why an animal presents a particular behaviour.

If only humans were open-minded enough to trust that we have the capability of tuning into our animals naturally, our relationship with them would reach unbelievable heights. Ever had that gut feeling that something doesn't feel right? That is your intuition at work!

Intuitive communication allows us to ask an animal how he is feeling physically, or, more profoundly, help him release emotional trauma - much of which he may have held for great lengths of time. Emotional trauma manifests negative behaviours, which can't be 'trained' out of the horse. Be aware that horses can and do take on board all our negative thoughts and emotions, many of which are capable of manifesting as physical ailments.

I appreciate you may not wish to be coaxed from your comfort zone or implanted beliefs that we are limited in how we can communicate with horses, and our other animal species.

I would not presume to push intuitive communication down your throat. Maybe you were not aware of this level of communication until now. Maybe you would rather stick with traditional methods. Perhaps your scepticism, fear, or any misguided beliefs you may hold prevent you delving into the unknown.

However, how will you now choose to use this new information? Will you take it upon yourself to study the evidence that is freely available to you online? Will you take it a step further and dare to enrol on an animal communication workshop? You have absolutely nothing to lose, but everything to gain. You have a potentially powerful source within you - the potential to truly communicate with the horses in your care. You require only an open and willing mind, and a teacher to nurture you. The animals in your care want you to take the leap of faith. They want to be able to communicate their problems and their joys to you without having to resort to dangerous physical actions. Are you really the responsible carer you portray yourself to be, who only wants the best for your horse?

I urge you to begin to question why a horse behaves in a particular way instead of conforming to the normal mindset that it is misbehaviour; the cause, rather than merely the symptom, may then be treated.

The reasons for a horse's behaviour and his vocal and body language when being ridden, form the backdrop of this guide.

You may be of the opinion that you need to read no further because you have come up through the training systems unscathed; you and your horse are doing pretty well in your chosen discipline, or you simply indulge in pleasure hacking. So I ask you this: how often have you taken short cuts with the use of gadgets when training a horse? How often do you say or hear the misguided command **Get him on the bit**? How many times have you used a gadget to keep the horse's mouth closed? How often have you actually considered how the horse may be feeling emotionally, mentally, and physically, when he is essentially manipulated into submission without his consent?

For all you cynics out there, I give you the following advice:

Open mindedness sets you free from the clutches of archaic, systematic training systems that continue to brainwash equestrians, at the expense of the wellbeing and true potential of both you and the horse. As soon as you are humble enough to question, you will begin to see a world full of possibilities, not limitations.

At all times when in the company of horses, it is vital that you have at the very least, calmness about you that the horses will notice and enjoy. Don't let the horses in your company take responsibility for your own emotional baggage; leave it all at the gate, keeping your mind sufficiently clear to allow you to remain completely focused in the present moment an aspect I will discuss further on.

Your relationship with the horse will improve if you are aware that he thrives much better when learning if you consider his natural instinct and preservation button. It is important you recognise that horses should be 'assisted' in their learning processes rather than 'trained'.

The process of teaching a horse must be on his terms without mental and physical restraint; he must have choices, the time to process each step at his pace. You must be prepared to stop, wait, and listen to him before further progression. Regrettably, impatient humans don't consider the horse has needs; they want a quick fix with the use of gadgets.

There is no place for punishment in the company of a horse. Confusion, tension, and misery will incapacitate him. Kicking with the legs and pulling on the reins when riding will cause discomfort, pain and a lack of confidence, resulting in a horse that appears to be unwilling and naughty.

It is so simple to ask him to move without kicking him, to stop him without touching the reins, and to slow him down simply by thinking *"slow"*! What a godsend, particularly when coaching beginner and novice riders, who should not have access to the reins until they are able to balance themselves on the horse.

We spend vast amounts of money shipping our horses off for re-schooling due to 'behavioural problems' they have suddenly developed. The horse is very soon back on track due to the skill and expertise of the professional. When he is returned to his regular handler, he may very soon begin to 'misbehave' again, because the expert has merely treated the symptoms; the cause (the regular handler) remains.

There certainly is no point in 'retraining' a horse if the handler persists in her habit of incorrectness, because the horse will continue to react to the bad handling and rider faults. The handler must be a willing participant in the rehabilitation process.

When riding, you must focus on using yourself correctly so that your posture, position, and connections naturally influence the horse, while at the same time, listening to his reactions to your posture, position, and connections.

If you don't notice his reaction, how can you recognise his subtle hints that something is wrong? Ignore him at your peril!

It is my mission to arm you with a 'white flag' to bring about a ceasefire between you and your horse when in the saddle.

My background

An insight into the author's life, from her beginnings of riding ponies truly free – pony and rider feeling and knowing what the other was asking – to qualifying as a BHSAI. She oozes passion and commitment as she shares her life-changing journey; a journey that would lead to a more profound level of communicating with horses and animals of all kinds through intuitive animal communication and reiki; a journey that became the catalyst for *Horse Riding in the 21st Century* - the revised edition of her earlier written work.

I am a British Horse Society Assistant Instructor with many years' experience in the horse industry, teaching freelance and in BHS approved Equestrian Centres, as well as for the Pony Club.

Along with starting, schooling, and rehabilitating horses, I have coached riders of all ages and abilities, from pleasure riders to competition riders.

I was renowned in the area I grew up for being fearless and able to 'sort a horse out' where others had failed. How sad I was given this title, merely because the handlers had confused, forced, tricked, and punished their horses when they didn't understand what was asked of them.

At around eight years old, I would without any thought jump on the nearest pony to hand and ride around the paddock - when no one was around - in any pace and direction I asked for; none of the ponies I encountered seemed to mind!

I didn't know how or why the ponies did as I asked; neither did I realise I was actually asking them to do anything. I simply remember that I would have a thought of wanting the pony to go in a particular direction and at a certain pace, and it would miraculously happen - most of the time.

Alas, the owner of a pony I had proudly named Monty, found me riding him one day. She was amazed that he allowed me to sit on his back, let alone without a saddle and a bridle. She let me into the fact that she hadn't ridden him for some time, as he had developed the nasty habit of bucking and rearing. Now being aware that he was quite happy to have a rider on his back, she would allow me to borrow his tack.

The change in his manner was dire. He was no longer willing to do as I asked. He no longer enjoyed our time together and to begin with, I failed to hear and understand what he was trying to tell me. But being an inquisitive youngster, and most unhappy that my friend seemed to have turned against me, I began to experiment with the tack; on, off, saddle placed on the withers, below the withers, girth tighter, looser - oops that one didn't work! I rode him bareback. He was almost back to his old self but there was still something amiss.

Hmm, if it wasn't the saddle, what could it be? I set about the bridle. I noticed that each time I tried something, I somehow understood the pony's body language when he appeared to say, *"Yep that's ok"* or *"Get that off me NOW!"* We once again enjoyed our time together, but I would always ride him bareback. After a while, his owner once again placed the saddle on his back; the pony objected with a capital 'O'! Monty's pain was obvious. He taught me the consequences of not listening to his kind.

Over the years, I had the opportunity of studying a large herd of horses living a natural lifestyle on marshland close to where I lived in Yorkshire. Their tranquil world literally drew me in; taking note of the vast range of vocabulary that appeared to have another jargon within it; their mannerisms, the mutual respect within the herd, the family ties, and the magnificent challenges and submissions were extraordinary. There was even a metaphorical 'naughty step' for the youngsters when they misbehaved.

When I started my first job at 16 years old, I saved my wages to buy my very own youngster. He was ten months old and very cheeky. I was a typical stroppy know it all teenager, and very hormonal.

To begin with, Trampus obviously thought of me as just 'one of the gang'. As he grew older, he was full of testosterone! A hormonal female and a colt was **not** a good match to begin with.

Advice was coming at me from all sides: ***"He needs a good beating", "Tie him up short"***. Thankfully, I took the advice from the herd of horses with which I had spent years learning. I had learned how the mares chastised their offspring. I used the same method with my colt; simple: no anger and certainly no pain or fear; it worked!

Trampus grew into a magnificent horse and we were always in the rosettes. However, I wasn't particularly interested in competing or going out there to win. I was more passionate about the correct learning process and welfare of the horse.

No instructor could ever match up to what the horse has taught me, without charge, ridicule, aggression, or trickery. Those magnificent masters taught me a lifelong lesson – **learning is a lifelong experience!**

My own experiences have taught me - **ignore your horse at your peril or at his suffering.**

1

A new beginning

The author discusses how, because we unwittingly deny the horse his basic right to be happy, we also risk our own safety. Two-way communication is essential if we are to bring out the best in our horses with the simplest of connections and very little effort while at the same time eliminating unnecessary punishment. ***Is my horse misbehaving?*** One of the numerous questions the author lists in her goal to plant the seed of reasoning. Her own answer ***"That depends on how you interpret misbehaviour"***, leads into specific scenarios that can either resign the horse to punishment, or find the support he needs.

The needs of the horse must always come first if our safety as riders is to be paramount! We have a greater chance of maintaining our own safety if our horses are safe and happy too.

Yet we sometimes unwittingly deny him this basic right. In neglecting his needs, we also risk our safety.

Two-way communication is essential if we are to bring out the best in our horses with the simplest of connections and very little effort, whilst also eliminating unnecessary punishment. We must remember that our ways are extremely alien to the horse.

The early identification and treatment of the root cause of a fault or problem is essential if harmony is to exist. Merely treat the symptom, the problem will remain. For example, a symptom of a horse with discomfort due to the saddle may be a buck, with a diagnosis of **disobedience**. Will you treat the symptom with a smack or a kick on his belly, or will you find the root cause and eliminate both? Of course, he may buck due to excitement, fear, or even possibly anger, none of which deserves a reprimand.

Unfortunately, all too often forgotten are the needs of the horse. Until recently, the information provided in formalised education was about horse care, his management, and equestrian skills. Information based on the mind of the horse seemed to be secondary, with the leaking of a little more information as the rider gained more knowledge in the other areas.

It is quite frustrating, because regardless of the age or ability of equestrians, the horse will still be a complicated animal with which to bond, if we don't learn to communicate with him on an equal level rather than as a subordinate, as is all too often the case. Below is a prime example of the lack of understanding we have towards our horses.

The traditional approach to, for example, dealing with a horse who refused a fence was to **make him do it**, although he probably refused it because he was frightened, in pain - all manner of things beyond his control. Therefore, a downward spiral would begin. The horse would begin to associate a fence with pain and he would try to avoid it at all costs, becoming more afraid as his rider tried to **make him do it**.

Although they were terrified of being whipped and kicked by their riders, some horses appeared to learn that if they cantered towards the fence and over it as fast as possible, the riders wouldn't whip them as long and as hard. However, the horses would then feel the pain of the aggressive pull on the reins as they landed, by riders anchoring their feet into the stirrups to get more pulling power on the reins. The horses could **not** win. Children grew up with the philosophy of pure dominance, passing it on to other unsuspecting beginner horse riders.

Awareness is improving over time;' I am confident that the physical, mental, and emotional abuse that presently goes unrecognised by those riders, handlers, trainers and judges who still remain fixed in the 20th century, will one day succumb to the 21st century ethics of being with horses.

Frequently, riders are told they must constantly correct a fault, with an indication of how to achieve a correction.

Many faults are impossible to correct unless your body motion mimics exactly the body motion of the horse. This will not be possible unless you are balanced and your lower body becomes a part of the horse. Yet I am conscious of many riders who remain unaware.

I have often heard the phrase *once you are on board, the horse must learn to re-balance himself.* How can he unless you are also balanced?

Are you conscious of the way your horse moves, or do you simply see him put one leg in front of the other when in motion?

When first learning to ride, were you encouraged to kick or squeeze with your legs to ask the horse to move his legs, to pull or squeeze on the reins to make him stop, to open and slightly pull back the inside rein if turning a corner, and to move your outside leg back to ask for canter?

Do you know the precise moment to use a particular leg or shift your weight?

It is true that the educated horse will usually go forward into canter when you move your outside leg further back, because he knows this is what he should do when he feels repetitions of particular pressures. Horses learn by repetition and association.

It doesn't necessarily imply that your leg has influenced him correctly. Many horses will pick up the canter on the incorrect lead when ridden by novice riders, even the more experienced, if the correct signal is not given.

As a rider, do you know how to achieve improvements? If you give a particular 'aid' and the horse doesn't respond, does your eye see what is not right? Can you feel what is not right? Do you have the knowledge and physical ability to try another technique, or do you find yourself giving the same signal time after time, hoping the horse will **get it**, because your knowledge is limited and that is the procedure which all the books describe?

If you feel you are flogging a dead horse – pardon the pun - I am confident you will get past your block if you experiment with the following guidance, and learn to listen to him. Experiment with various body, seat, leg, and hand positions, being sure to take notice of how your horse reacts. You can learn much by watching him.

Too many riders who fail to obtain correctness from their horses listen to the advice of other 'unenlightened experts' - *"He needs a stronger bit"* or *"He needs a flash noseband to prevent him from opening his mouth"*, or *"You must wear spurs to wake him up"*.

You must always question why gadgets are used and look for the best possible alternative solution. Be honest with yourself; you must never fit a gadget just because other riders use it.

Can you recognise incorrectly fitted tack, which may be the cause of many problems in the horse and you as the rider?

Many riders have limited patience when confronted by horses that are unable to achieve a good result. The rider very often blames her lack of tolerance on the horse's misbehaviour. However, as you read on, you will learn that obvious negative influences beyond the control of both you and your horse can prevent both from working correctly, but for which a reprimand is given by a rider who is blind to the signs.

My gift to you

I would like you to accept the following valuable gift of the five precepts, created by Mikao Usui, the founder of the Reiki system that I live by as an Equine Reiki Master Practitioner, and in all other aspects of my life. I ask that you learn them, say each precept to yourself each morning, and certainly prior to your riding session. I am confident that your personal life and schooling sessions will run considerably more smoothly. Pass the precepts on to your friends and notice the positive transformation in the emotional, mental, and physical wellbeing of both horse and rider.

JUST FOR TODAY:

■ *Do not anger:* it can sometimes be frustrating when your signals don't appear to be getting across to your horse. Embedding this precept in your mind will serve as a reminder that frustration and anger breed only negative results.

■ *Do not worry:* the positive energy emitted through you to your horse when you believe in yourself as a human being and a rider, can be unbelievably strong. Any worries you may have to begin with simply drift away, relieving the horse of any plans he has to flee the negative energy.

■ **Be humble:** mistaking ego for self-confidence will result in your downfall and the horse's lack of respect for you. Create positive energy in being proud of your achievements. The positive vibes resound all around. Boasting of how good you are will create resentment and negative energy.

■ **Be honest in your dealings with others: 'Honesty is always the best policy',** as the saying goes. It is certainly the best policy when around horses. When riding, you have to be honest with yourself; admit your limitations, don't be tempted to ride out of your capabilities.

Always be honest with the horse; for example, don't be afraid to let the horse know if you are lacking in confidence. Trying to hide emotions from the horse will cause him to doubt and mistrust you. Keep the horse in the picture at all times; after all, he is taking part in the proceedings.

■ **Be compassionate to yourself and others:** don't beat yourself up if things don't go according to plan. Don't beat the horse up (metaphorically or otherwise) when he doesn't understand your directions. The horse deserves your utmost courtesy and understanding. Learning how to keep negative energy at bay, and oozing a positive and calming energy in all aspects of your life, will enhance your wellbeing and that of the horses in your company.

Is my horse misbehaving?

That depends on how you interpret misbehaviour. The Dictionary defines misbehaviour as **unacceptable behaviour especially naughtiness, disobedience or troublesomeness**.

If you crept up quietly from behind a horse, touched his bottom and he kicked out because you startled him, would that be **unacceptable**?

If you approached directly from the front, touched his head and he spooked because you were standing in his blind spot and he could not see you, threw his head up, possibly unwittingly hitting you, would that be **naughtiness**?

If, without warning, you touched his back and he bucked, barged, or reared because he thought you would eat him, would that be **disobedience**?

If he spooked at a gremlin in the bushes, or where the light changed, would that be **misbehaviour**?

If you answered yes to any of the above questions, my guess is that the horse was punished, and branded as unpredictable and unsafe.

If a normally quiet horse suddenly bucks, rears, or bolts while under saddle, is he to be punished for being in pain, frightened or confused? On the other hand, will you now listen to him, as his gentle hints were unheard?

A whole host of reasons - discussed further on - come to mind why he may appear to misbehave. As a rider and handler of horses, you have an obligation to understand how he ticks in every way. How can you respond positively if you don't know when he is unsure of something, when he is in pain, or what he is asking of you?

The horse's eyesight can have much to do with his behaviour. His eyes are set to the side of his face. He can tell we are predators due to our eyes being to the front of our faces and closer together. He has learned to trust that we don't knowingly wish to harm him, but on occasions, the horse does feel the need to watch our every move, and that of other predatory animals, if he is to keep himself safe.

Like humans, he has binocular vision; he can see the same scene as us, but because his eyes are set to the side of his head his peripheral vision gives him a completely different perspective.

He also has monocular vision; he can see separate pictures with each eye. He tends to use his monocular vision when grazing, relaxing, and when out for a leisurely hack, but because his large eyes are so sensitive to movement, his monocular vision also gives him the tendency to spook, particularly on windy days when there is a lot of movement.

Although the horse has remarkable all round vision due to his long and flexible neck, he has a blind spot directly in front of his face and he is unable to see his own chest and front legs. He has to raise his head to enable him to see close objects, such as when we suddenly appear in front of him. He must lower his head to enable him to see objects at a distance and in an attempt to judge the depth of an object, for example, when jumping.

He has a blind spot directly behind him and above him; he is unable to see a rider on his back when his head is facing ahead. These blind spots can be a cause of spooking.

The horse will usually use monocular vision when ridden by beginner and novice riders who are not capable of achieving his concentration, so you must be aware of his tendency to spook.

When a horse is working in an outline and his head is on or just in front of the vertical, the poll flexion removes his ability to see ahead, his focus is downwards to the ground, resulting in his binocular vision coming into play.   Unfortunately, for him, it also boosts the blind spot in front of his face. He must then rely on his rider to guide him – how trusting is that?

His eyes need time to adjust to varying lighting, such as going from sunlight into shadow.

If he isn't allowed to lift or lower his head when he asks, or be given time to come to terms with everything thrown at him, he will probably panic and refuse to go forward, or buck, rear, bolt, bite - anything to get rid of the gremlin.

An uneducated coach or rider will no doubt reach a conclusion of misbehaviour, and will punish him, a battle neither the rider nor coach will win!

When a horse reacts badly, the following possibilities must be considered:

- Is his tack ill fitting?

- Is he reacting to you, his rider?

- Is there a less obvious reason for his behaviour?

Does he (a) - react badly to another rider but is absolutely fine with you or does he (b) - appear to misbehave with most if not all riders; if the answer is (a) it will probably be rider error. If the answer is (b) the reason could be ill-fitting tack, soreness/discomfort, fear of his surroundings, excitement, feeling out of sorts, or he may be on the road to depression; he may be bored with a mundane daily routine, he may need stimulation and variety, or he simply can't be bothered!

The subject of correctly fitted tack is discussed in depth further in the guide.

A horse may not be cut out for the type of discipline and life you have made for him. He should be heard when he begins to give subtle hints of his distaste.

If a horse feels the vibes of a rider who is not quite up to scratch, he may become stubborn and slow; he may playfully take the reins from his rider's hands. On the other hand, if he feels ill at ease, his survival instinct will kick in; he will take action to establish dominance over the weak willed. The frustrated rider may start to kick hard or pull on the reins as she becomes tense and agitated. A fight has begun that the rider will not win. The horse will simply dig in his heels.

The recognition of a human who is brave, kind, confident and respectful, will instil the same in the horse. There will be only rider and horse communicating naturally, without the need for war! Never place a horse in a position where he feels he has to test your physical and emotional strength.

A horse accustomed to constantly having an unbalanced stiff rider on his back, will eventually learn to ignore the imperfection; he will mimic the stiffness and will become one sided and unbalanced.

A well-schooled and balanced horse will immediately object to an unbalanced and stiff rider; he will drift from the uneven weight. The rider will have difficulty keeping him on the track and may not succeed in asking him to move off from the halt. The rider's imperfection, however small, can be detrimental in the extreme to the movement and behaviour of the horse. However, the rider may misunderstand his reluctance to obey as **disobedience**.

2

Anatomy enlightenment

The horse was not designed to be ridden! The author has concerns that riders and handlers of varying ability are not always au-fait with the location, operation, and possible detriment of the horse's anatomy. She offers a much-needed basic, yet informative insight into the temporomandibular joint, hyoid bone, atlas, the ribs in relation to the shoulder, nuchal and supraspinous ligaments and the latissimus dorsi muscle. The signs, effects, and simple checking procedures of the one sided horse are discussed, as are the damaging effects of feeding the horse from a hay net.

The horse was not designed to be ridden! The development of the longissimus dorsi muscle was to aid the horse's motion, not to take the vertical weight of a rider. If you are not yet convinced of the torture the horse suffers at the hands of bad riders and handlers, maybe the brief and simple examples given below will sway you in his favour. They will, I hope, cause you to re-think how you handle a horse, ride, feed him, and possibly coach a rider.

The temporomandibular joint

The TMJ lies between the eye and base of the ear; it is where the jaw joins the skull. It is a site of pain that frequently goes undetected.

Lots of ligaments, muscles, and tendons support it; therefore, its proper alignment and function is vital to the good health of the horse, his stability, and his movement. Any dysfunction or restriction of the jaw will prevent the horse from carrying his head naturally. The imbalance will mirror through his neck and in turn, throughout his body. His muscles will deteriorate.

There are many causes for its dysfunction, ranging from an untreated dental problem, stress in other areas of his body, simply banging his head, to abusive bits, nosebands, and other gadgets.

Is your horse able to yawn or does he appear to struggle? Maybe he gives a half –hearted yawn. Take notice, because a possible indicator of pain in the TMJ is a half-hearted yawn. Sometimes you may also be able to hear the joint clicking when the horse is chewing.

More signs of problems

- The appearance of stiffness in the horse's neck or back.

- Twisting, shaking, and tossing his head.

- The reins feel heavy in your hands.

- The reins are almost continuously pulled from your hands.

- Bucking, rearing, bolting and so on.

The above signs are all too often misdiagnosed as **disobedience**, an **ill-fitting saddle**, and quite often, a change of bit is advised because the horse obviously isn't happy with the one in use!

How to check for soreness in the TMJ

The TMJ lies in the area where the brow band normally attaches to each cheek piece of the bridle. You will recognise the joint of the mandible by a bony protrusion between the eye and the ear.

From each bone, down the side of the horse's face towards the mouth, runs a nerve. When pressed just under the bony protrusion, the horse should show no reaction if it is problem free. However, he will react if there is soreness.

Ensuring your safety, stand in front of your horse and place an index finger directly on each protrusion. Are both finger points equal or does one appear to be lower than the other? You must ensure the horse's head is straight to begin with. If his head appears to tilt, that is a sure sign of some problem. Take a photo of the horse's head for proper scrutinising of possible deformities. The power of the camera is discussed further on!

Do **not** ignore the horse's reaction. You must have him checked out by a vet who has knowledge of the TMJ and its problems.

You will find throughout this guide that the horse will present the same symptoms for a large spectrum of problems. However, the guide's supervision and numerous checklists will hold your hand through a process of elimination.

As you narrow the symptoms down, your eyes and open-mindedness will have more clarity! Spurred on, you may even hit the nail on the head. At the very least, you will now be extremely sensitive to where the problem probably lies. You will now have the knowledge needed to seek the relevant expert help.

The hyoid bone

The hyoid bone is part of a group of bones all playing a part in the TMJ mechanism. It is an attachment point for the ligaments and muscles of the tongue, pharynx, neck, and sternum.

It is immobile and unable to move backwards to alleviate the pressure of the bit on the tongue. Over flexing the horse's neck places exceeding amounts of pressure on his tongue, forcing the back of it to rise up into an arch. This in turn makes it difficult for him to breathe and relax his jaw.

Imagine the hyoid bone is a chicken wishbone. Imagine the finger with which you pull the wishbone is the tongue being forced back onto the hyoid bone. Need I say more?

The muscles in the forehand lose their mobility because they too attach from the sternum to the hyoid bone. However, it doesn't end there. If the horse is constrained in his forehand, he will be restricted through his whole body.

The atlas

The atlas, otherwise known as the first cervical vertebrae, connects to the back of the skull and holds the horse's head up; another site of pain and injury that goes unnoticed.

Pain will be a negative consequence of a head pulled or forced into an unnatural position. The horse's stiffness and resistance may be misinterpreted as an evasion.

The ribs in relation to the shoulder

Because the horse has no clavicle as a solid frame for the rib cage, the ribs are quite vulnerable in their instability. Its absence allows for greater rotation of the scapula and a good length of stride. However, pain and injuries around the area often manifest as lameness, resulting in the misdiagnosis of foot lameness.

The first rib sits in front of the scapula; it can become easily displaced causing pain and restriction in the scapula, resulting in compensations throughout the body. The second rib lies against the scapula. Restriction of the horse's head and neck can generate so much tension on the second rib that inflammation and swelling can often be seen along the length of the front of the scapula.

The nuchal and supraspinous ligaments

The nuchal ligament is a very strong elastic cord. Its origin is at the poll; it runs down the length of the neck to the spinous processes of the withers. It supports the horse's head, neck, and helps him to balance himself.

Thick fibrous strands fan out and attach to each of the cervical vertebrae giving further stability.

On reaching the withers, the nuchal ligament fuses with the supraspinous ligament that runs the length over the spinous processes of the thoracic and lumbar vertebrae, to the sacrum. The spinous processes form the bumpy ridge that can be felt along the middle of the horse's back.

The supraspinous ligament is designed to lift and support the horse's back. It also helps support the gut contents. When the horse's head and neck are stretched forward and down, his back is raised by the forward pull on the spinous processes by the nuchal ligament.

They play a vital part in the horse's balance and motion, particularly when he is carrying your weight. When functioning efficiently, these two ligaments allow the back muscles to pay more attention to the propulsion than support.

The longissimus dorsi muscle

Being the largest and longest muscle in the horse's back, it is the connecting bridge between the hindquarters and the front of the horse. Being a powerful extensor muscle, it also aids the limited lateral flexion of the spine.

It supports the ligaments in carrying the gut contents, and, along with the other back muscles, it propels and allows the energy to follow its natural course from the hindquarters, through the back, along the neck to the poll, and finally to your hands.

However, if the supraspinous ligament is not sufficiently strong, the horse will attempt to use his back muscles to support your weight which can be extremely tiring for him. The restriction and possible soreness will result in a hollow back, and the loss of propulsion.

In his natural habitat, the long grazing hours will result in a good strong back with well-developed muscles to propel the horse forward when necessary.

The same luxury is often neglected in the human environment due to restrictions on the horse's natural way of life.

It is crucial that the horse is free to lower his head and neck to the ground as often as possible if he is to take advantage of his upper ligament system to maintain his strength. He will need it when he has your added weight bearing down on him.

When the horse has the freedom to stretch his top line muscles, he must also be encouraged to engage the antagonist muscles of the lower abdomen and the flexor muscles.

Exercises such as the use of ground poles will encourage the horse to engage his hindquarters. Groundwork including carrot stretches will encourage him to lift and strengthen the lower stomach muscles.

The one sided horse

There is a general understanding that, like humans, horses come into the world already armed with a dominant side preference: he is naturally left or right handed. Left to his own devices, the horse will remain one-sided. This would be of no concern to him; his crookedness would not affect his ability to flee a predator.

There are various means of determining the horse's 'side' preference. Current research shows that a horse with a clockwise flowing facial whorl is most likely to show right side preference and vice-versa.

The horse's crookedness may be relieved by working equally on both sides of his body. Crookedness ranges from minimal to off the scale. However, conformation faults, injury, lameness, an unbalanced rider and so on, can amplify his crookedness.

His crookedness prevents the horse from performing correctly under saddle, a burden often misinterpreted as evasion.

I am confident that our own musculoskeletal imbalanced manipulation and our lack of knowledge and consideration play a gigantic role in any one-sidedness he may suffer. For example:

- Persistent handling and leading from the left side results in weak, short and under developed muscles on the left side of the horse due to their constant contraction.

- As the muscles on the left side contract, they shorten and try to pull their attachments closer to each other. They also become thicker and change shape as the fibres bunch together. If the horse is not then encouraged to pull those attachments apart by contracting the muscles on the right side of his body, the left side muscles will remain contracted.

- In contrast the muscles on the right side receive a good workout. They are free to expand and grow strong.

- When the horse is asked to perform the same tasks on the right rein, the weak and underdeveloped muscles on his left side won't allow him the freedom to do so.

- He will appear to be stiff on his right rein, even though the problem is on his left side. Incorrect diagnosis may then identify the horse as right rein resistant and non-compliant.

- An inexperienced and/or lopsided rider, for her own ease, may then allow the horse to remain on the rein she finds he best performs.

I will use the right rein resistant horse as an example.

■ You are riding your horse in the arena on the left rein; turns, circles and transitions come easily and quite smoothly.

■ You change the rein across the long diagonal. As you head off onto the right rein, everything begins to fall apart!

■ The horse still appears to be bending his body around your left leg, with his head looking towards the fence, in spite of your desperate attempts to encourage him to do the opposite. He is now blocked between both your legs.

■ You attempt to turn his head to the inside; his response appears to be evasion of the bit.

■ He now begins to escape through his inside shoulder (right) as he moves further and further in from the outside track.

■ As your goal is to get the horse back to the outside track, you make a combined effort of steering him back there with your outside rein while your eyes fix firmly on the fence.

■ You fail miserably as the horse continues on his preferred route.

By now, you are probably frustrated, angry, disillusioned, and you may have punished the horse in some way for his disobedience.

The horse on the other hand, **did** try his best for you! Being imperfect is **not** his fault. His lack of muscle strength and suppleness is **not** in his control. However, although he may have become disillusioned, he would never think to punish you.

Very often, the horse is blamed for the rider's unbalance. You may not notice your unevenness on your own horse. He will constantly try to adjust his position to accommodate your unstable seat. A rider, uneven in her seat, will give the horse the signal to step in the direction of the seat bone bearing the most pressure. Are you sure that you are not the culprit?

Symptoms of right rein resistance

The horse's static and dynamic conformation should be examined, both from the ground and when ridden. A knowledgeable, sensitive rider should be able to feel the signs of rein preference and resistance, and the possible reasons. A left rein resistant horse will typically show opposite signs.

- The right shoulder muscle of a horse displaying right rein resistance may be visibly larger than the left shoulder muscle.

- The muscles in general covering his right side are often more developed than on his left side.

- His corresponding hip joints, hocks, knees, and so on may be out of alignment.

- The horse prefers to strike off on the left canter lead using his stronger right hind leg, because he is able to bend more easily to the left.

- He will place his right foreleg out in front when grazing more regularly than his left foreleg, to bear the weight of his dominant side.

- As the weight of his body bears down through his right fore-leg, it in turn puts pressure on the hoof, which will be wider and flatter than his opposite hoof, which will be upright.

- You may find that your horse shows reluctance to pick up his hind leg on the stronger side for the farrier, or to have his foot picked out, because he feels unable to balance himself properly on the weaker side. He may have pain in his sacral area or other area, which causes his varying degrees of reaction.

- Of course, he may show preference to one leg due to a genetic condition of the opposite hoof, which may appear upright and is causing problems for the horse.

■ Have you noticed how your horse's front hooves may differ in shape and size? Investigation into the possible reasons would be appropriate.

■ Ask your farrier for advice. A small deviation in the hooves can be normal but can quickly become a large problem if not attended to regularly by the farrier. A clubfoot may cover up much more than mere natural one-side preference. Always remember the saying **No foot, no horse.**

How to check your horse for uneven shoulder muscle development

■ Stand directly behind the horse at a safe distance, making sure he is standing square with his head and neck facing directly forward. The more lopsided the horse is, the less ability he may show in standing square.

■ Ensuring your head is centred, look along the length of his spine.

■ Any disparity in his left and right shoulder muscles will be clearly visible.

■ Any asymmetry in the muscles along his back and hindquarters must be noted and acted on accordingly. Essentially, seek expert advice to determine the reasons for the asymmetry; a plan of action will be necessary.

■ If your horse has uneven muscle development, for whatever reason, it is likely that your existing saddle doesn't fit him, unless it was made for purpose and is maintained. You should make a note of his 'behavioural problems' and begin to eliminate them!

A hay net is artillery. Surely not!

Feeding from the ground is crucial to the horse's wellbeing and correct muscle development. The design and weight of the horse's neck, head, and jaw set the downward direction for natural grazing, with gentle bending and lifting as required. He has natural drainage from his nose and the freedom to blow away any debris that threatens his nasal passage.

Feeding from a hay net or rack can have the following consequences:

■ The horse is forced to eat from a foreign angle, so he must adjust his posture to enable him to tug the hay from the net.

■ As he grabs a mouthful of hay, he must twist his head and neck as he draws back to make clearance from the net.

■ The abnormal position of the jaw as he tugs at the hay will cause uneven wear of the teeth. It may also result in nerve damage.

■ His back will hollow.

■ The muscles on the underside of the horse's neck will over-develop while the muscles along his top line and back will remain weak.

■ He will be unable to blow out any debris from his nose due to the position of his head, resulting in possible respiratory problems.

■ Hayseeds may fall into his eyes causing irritation, scratching, and soreness.

■ He won't have freedom of the full range of natural movement through his head and neck.

■ The horse may also develop behavioural problems due to the stress he faces while eating unnaturally.

If feeding from a hay net, consider the following:

■ Is the horse's head elevated - which will put his lower jaw out of alignment with the top jaw when eating;

■ Even if eating at lower levels is his head constantly at a foreign angle when eating.

When left to his own devices, the horse will forage in areas where he may occasionally need to elevate his head, or place it at a foreign angle to reach those juicy shoots under the fence. It is when we place the restrictions that constantly force him into unnatural positions, that we put his general health in jeopardy.

However we decide to feed hay, we must ensure it is as near to mimicking his natural feeding habits as possible. When you next put out your horse's hay, take the time to watch how he eats. If his head is down, and he can tug the hay as naturally as he tugs at the grass with very little head movement, then you are on the right track.

Assessment of the horse's mouth

To keep abreast of any possible dental problems, an assessment of the horse's mouth is ideally carried out on a daily basis. However, the task is often left for the equine dentist on scheduled visits.

Regular examination of the gums, inside the cheeks, the upper and lower palate, the bars, and the whole of the tongue for signs of cuts, bruises, ulcers, and other injuries is essential.

The inspection of the crevices of the gums is just as crucial but often neglected by horse owners.

I ponder that we all on occasions chew on a food that gets stuck between our gum and the lip or cheek. If we are unable to dislodge it with our tongue, we have a choice of fingers to help us out. If lodged between the teeth, we have toothpicks.

Dental problems can occur very easily in horses when food, such as chewed grass and bits of grain get stuck between the crevices of the gums. Grain and seeds can easily dig into the sensitive tissues. If the skin is broken, open sores and abscesses may result.

The horse has no tools to dislodge the irritation. In an attempt to make you aware of his dilemma, the horse may rub his mouth on you. If you ignore him, he will try to rub the discomfort on his leg, maybe on his stable door. As he rubs, he will exacerbate the problem.

Add the bit, a tight noseband, and a flash to prevent him opening his mouth as he continues to fight with the alien lodged within it. What can he do now in a last ditch attempt to alert you to his pain? He may start to toss his head. You may decide an added gadget may keep him in check.

His evasions will escalate, yet it would have taken but a few seconds to ensure the horse was comfortable and clean in his mouth prior to putting on his bridle.

It is also crucial that you examine for any unusual heat or swelling around his jaw and face. Any unevenness or sensitivity in the masseter muscles, his forehead or around the base of his ears could indicate a dental problem.

Look out for any abnormalities in the alignment of the incisors, which can be due to dysfunction of the TMJ.

3

Evasion – Part 1:
Our artillery

You will discover when probing into the reasons for
the horse's evasion, that we are often the opponents
as we lead our horses on an inadvertent path of
destruction. We have the innate ability to transform
our natural aids into built in artillery, all of which
boost the influence of the other arms at our disposal.
Sound practical advice opens up your mind to the
simple options leading to harmony.

The term 'evasion' pops up frequently in the equestrian
world. Although it encompasses the whole spectrum of
avoidance by the horse in every area of his life, many
equestrians usually associate evasion only in the ridden sense,
such as evasion of the bit, evasion of the rider's leg, and so on.

Unless the horse has been with you since birth, you may not
be aware of any mental, emotional or physical trauma he has
suffered, such as a painful experience with a previous farrier.
As soon as he sees and hears familiar tools, he may panic as
he relives the emotional, painful experience. Various signs of
evasion may manifest such as pulling back on the tie rope,
kicking out, and attempts to rear and so on.

Riding school horses must be as safe and as well behaved as possible, but it takes just one unsavoury memory to trigger his flight instinct, and he will take evasive action.

Admittedly, sometimes his evasion is simply because he just can't be bothered. Just like us, horses have off days, days when they simply want to chill out with their friends or days when they feel under the weather. However, that is where the similarity with humans ends.

For example, if we are feeling under the weather, we have the choice of going into work but we may try to avoid putting any effort into a task, or we will 'throw a sickie'! We may also pretend we are ill if we don't want to go into work. We have free will.

The horse won't pretend; he will never try to pull the wool over our eyes. He will attempt to communicate his plight to us, often without success. He doesn't have free will, so he will go to work, but, hard as he may try, he won't give his best that day. His reward may be punishment.

Obviously, it would not be practical to allow school horses or other 'earners' the time off if they pass relevant health checks. Busy equestrians, trying to make a living with the help of their horses, often don't recognise their 'under the weather days'. However, showing these horses gratitude for what they do instead of handing out punishment for what they don't do, would be a step forward in the right direction.

The following content is based on evasions by the horse when ridden; however, it is essential that any 'shirking' by the horse be fully investigated.

Our artillery

The unwitting opponents

As unwitting opponents we set off a chain reaction in which the horse faces two choices – his first choice would be to bring his fight or flight instinct into play; his remaining choice is to submit. Either way we wound him.How the horse reacts depends on how badly we wound him physically, emotionally, mentally, and spiritually. Sadly, much of the time we are oblivious to the harm we inflict on him.

We have **built in artillery** such as our hands, legs, seat, negative energy, all of which boost the influence of the other arms at our disposal, whether an inanimate entity such as the bridle, bodily, such as our brute force, or psychological such as an anxious mind, anger, frustration, neglect, and our disrespect of the horse. He is effectively at our mercy.

We are solely responsible for our actions as opponents and the resulting reactions of the horse. Furthermore, we must take responsibility for our large arsenal store discussed below.

The bridle

I liken the bridle to a birdcage: the bird is locked behind bars from where there is no escape, but despite his restrictive prison, he still tries to sing sweetly.

It is a fact that people, who take into consideration the importance of a correctly fitted saddle, and the likely problems a poor fitting saddle can cause, don't always give the same importance to the fit of the bridle.

However, the consequences of a badly fitting bridle can cause discomfort at best; at its worst, it **will** cause physical and emotional trauma.

Attempts to put on the bridle may be met with resentment by the horse; he may present 'behavioural problems', which may become more apparent when the horse is ridden.

Bridles come with nosebands and bits offering various degrees of pressure and control.

Science now proves that the emotional and physical well-being and welfare of horses is much improved when ridden without a bit and restrictive nose-band. As responsible guardians of horses, we must acknowledge scientific evidence that will enable us to make the best choice for the horses in our care. If your choice is to remain with 20th century outdated tradition, I urge you to never consider changing to a more severe bit if your horse shows signs of evasion.

There is a valid reason for his behaviour. This aspect is discussed further on in this guide.

The bridle should fit the horse like a glove:

- The headpiece rests gently behind his ears on the poll; your finger is able to slide comfortably on the underside of the strap.

- The brow band sits on the forehead. It should sit straight and not be so small that it would tug where it attaches to the headpiece or touches the base of the ear, and not so large that it hangs down.

- The cheek straps are in alignment. If they are too long, the bit will hang low in the mouth and rest on the lower lip. The bit will also hit the horse's front teeth. Fastened too short, the bit will sit too high in the mouth and dig into the horse's cheeks; the bit will essentially pull back on the corners of the mouth showing very noticeable creases. Both scenarios would cause jarring and pain, not to mention deterioration in his mental state as the horse tries to bite down on, or push the bit forward in an attempt to alleviate the pain.

- When fitted, the bit protrudes out of each mouth corner so as avoid any pinching or the threat of pinching.

- The bit, no matter the type or size, will always cause discomfort.

- The throat lash is neither too tight when it will interfere with the horse's ability to breathe, nor too loose, when it will be of no use in preventing the headpiece from slipping over the ears.

- When fastened, it sits just under the jaw with allowance for the width of four fingers or your fist between the throat area and the throat lash.

- The throat lash is not secured by the top hole; if the throat lash becomes caught on an object and the horse pulls, the likeliest place for it to snap would be the hole on which the buckle is fastened.

- All corresponding straps are fastened equally.

- The cavesson noseband sits level across the horse's nose, one to two fingers width below the protruding cheekbone. It should **not** be fastened tightly.

The noseband

does what it says on the tin when used negligently.

- The cavesson noseband is the simplest type of noseband and has become more of a decorative piece of equipment over time; it plays no particular role other than for the attachment of a standing martingale. If worn, it **should** provide comfort without any restriction. When used even with the slightest negligence, the noseband has the capacity to reduce blood flow significantly and to crack the nasal bone!

- However, the over tightening of the cavesson noseband is often a deterrent against the horse opening his mouth too wide, or even worse, clamping his mouth **shut**. If his mouth were comfortable with the bit, he would **not** feel the need to open his mouth! The horse must be soft and relaxed in his mouth and jaw if he is to carry out his work to the best of his ability.

- The cavesson noseband sits closer and is at its tightest, **over the horse's nasal bone**. To carry out the 'two fingers' test at any other point around its circumference would give a false and detrimental reading. Two adult fingers must fit quite comfortably between the leather and the bone.

ISES (International Society for Equitation Science) has kindly given me written consent to insert a copy of its 2012 website posting of the following Position Statement of Restrictive Nosebands, the content of which epitomises the principles given in this guide. The use of the taper gauge as given in the RECOMMENDATION of the ISES Position Statement is so far proving to be inefficient. The 'adult two fingers test' remains the best option in my opinion; ensuring all round comfort and space between the nose and the noseband is a must.

> "Extreme tightening of the noseband may force the mucous membranes lining the cheek against the molar teeth and is thought to increase the bitted horse's compliance and responsiveness to rein pressure, perhaps by sensitising its mouth (Randle & McGreevy, 2011). This may advantage the rider since the horse appears to achieve a lighter rein contact, colloquially referred to as becoming more 'submissive'. However, tightening the noseband is likely to mask the horse's natural comfort-seeking responses by restricting jaw and tongue movements that disclose resistance and behavioural conflict.
>
> Recent evidence suggests that horses wearing tight nosebands undergo a physiological stress response, are sensitised to bit pressure and may have reduced blood flow (McGreevy et al., 2012). Consequently, on welfare grounds, the use of nosebands that constrict with potential to cause injuries should not be permitted in training or competition.
>
> Tight nosebands can mask unwanted behaviour in horses, which might be indicative of either pain or deficiencies in training, or, indeed, both. Consequently, the loosening of nosebands might reveal undesirable responses that could be dangerous to riders and other horse-rider combinations. Riders should therefore rule out any pain-related issues in their horses and ensure that their horses are trained according to principles of learning theory to meet the demands of competition.
>
> In most equestrian disciplines, gear stewards check that all equipment used on horses competing complies

with the specified regulations. By implementing a process that can be used to remove or loosen tight nosebands, stewards could ensure that the detrimental effects of these devices could be eliminated or at least lessened.

Furthermore, it is an established principle of ethical equitation that the horse's relaxation must be benchmarked (McGreevy & McLean, 2007; ISES, 2011). This entails training lightness of rein contact by carefully eliminating expressions of mouth discomfort such as opening, gaping or crossing the jaw. Indeed, in the same vein, some equestrian manuals and competition rule books propose that 'two fingers' be used as a spacer to guard against over-tightening, but fail to specify where this gauge should be applied or, indeed, the size of the fingers. The dimensions of average adult first and index fingers at the second joint are 1.59 × 3.87 × 9.89 cm (McGreevy et al., 2012).

This amount of space under the noseband allows horses to express conflict behaviour and so aligns with the principles of ethical equitation. That said, it does not permit horses to perform the full repertoire of behaviours, including yawning (McGreevy et al, 2012).

RECOMMENDATION

ISES recommends that all equestrian sports should require that the tightness of any noseband is checked by a steward at the nasal midline.

For fairness and objectivity, a taper gauge inserted under the noseband should be used for this purpose. The gauge should be placed without force and be clearly marked to show the desired stop, which, in alignment with established industry guidance, should be the dimensions of two average adult fingers. Riders should be advised and encouraged to use the same gauge in practice.

REFERENCES

ISES (The International Society for Equitation Science) 2011. Training principles:

does your training system stand the test of science? http://www.equitationscience.com/news.html. Accessed 7th Dec 2011. McGreevy P.D., McLean, A.N. 2007. The roles of learning theory and ethology in equitation. Journal of Veterinary Behavior: Clinical Applications and Research. 2, 108-118.

McGreevy, P., Warren-Smith, A., Guisard, Y. 2012. The effect of double bridles and jaw-clamping crank nose-bands on facial cutaneous and ocular temperature in horses. Journal of Veterinary Behavior: Clinical Applications and Research. Accepted.

Randle, H., McGreevy, P.D. 2011. The effect of noseband tightness on rein tension in the ridden horse. Proceedings of the 7th International Equitation Science Conference, Eds: M. van Dierendonck, P. de Cocq, K. Visser, Wageningen Academic Publishers, Wageningen. 84."

Constantly and repeatedly shackled at his nose by a tight noseband, or through his mouth, head and neck from an ill-fitting bit, or through his back by a saddle that pinches for long periods, inevitably results in the build-up of the horse's emotional state to such an extent that at the slightest hint of freedom, such as loosening of the noseband or girth, he may erupt like a volcano.

At the loosening of his shackles, the horse will not consider the relief he feels at that precise moment. He will only remember the repeated pressure and just this once, he has the chance to escape; in an instant, the magma will uncontrollably flow! He will now be unable to listen to anything you have to say to him. He may be punished; he may be shipped off for 'retraining', or even sold to the highest bidder as unpredictable.

These scenarios could be a thing of the past if we humans would recognise the scientifically proven natural energetic connection we have with the horses in our care; a connection that allows us to delve deeper than the physical horse that stands before us.

The flash noseband

The flash strap of the noseband is threaded through the attachment at the front of the cavesson noseband. It comes around and below the bit, through the chin groove, and back up towards its buckle. Once fastened, the spare leather is secured through the attachment. Although the flash noseband was 'created to hold the bit steady' in the horse's mouth, it is frequently wrongly recommended to keep the mouth closed lower down to prevent the horse crossing his jaw, and to prevent him putting his tongue over the top of the bit. Equestrians ought to be asking, *"Why is my horse evading the rein"* instead of asking, *"Which restrictive piece of equipment will work the best"*!

The flash strap should not be fastened near the mouth or nostrils.

- Place the middle finger of each hand on your nasal bone; let each index finger rest just lower down; place each thumb under your chin.

- Push up with your thumbs and down with your fingers with varying degrees of pressure in various areas of your nose and under the chin. Restrict your nasal passage a little.

- Now go and collect your bridle, take off the flash noseband, burn it at the stake, pour yourself a celebratory beverage and give a toast to a new future and friendship with your horse, as you destroy this abusive **gadget**.

Until you finally begin to realise the potential damage caused by these contraptions, a drop noseband or grackle noseband would be far better than the cavesson used with the flash, as they would not increase the pressure in the mouth or around the lips and mouthpiece to the same extent as a flash.

That being said, these nosebands can also be dangerous when combined with a rider with heavy hands. The horse may object to the drop noseband as it sits lower down on the nose than the flash.

The martingale

You may have a running or standing martingale in your tack room. They have always been extremely popular for better control of the horse: to prevent him from throwing his head up above the level of control, to help keep his head down for a better outline, and, because the young rider thinks it 'looks good'.

This device directs the pull of the reins placing more leverage on the bit and forcing the horse to lower his head when he lifts it higher than the rider requires. It is unwisely considered a temporary training aid; it is also recklessly used as a safety device for a rider who would otherwise be unable to control the horse or pony. Are you aware, that due to the leverage on the bit, the running martingale should not be used in conjunction with a curb bit? Yet, I have come across riders who have not only combined the two, but who have attached the fork straps of the martingale to the reins of the curb bit!

The use of training aids such as draw reins, running reins, the market Harborough and the pessoa, will never be a substitute for time, patience, correct exercises to build correct posture and muscle mass, and allowing the horse to go at his own pace in his learning process.

However, I do believe that like humans, horses may need a little extra artificial assistance in rehabilitation from injury. An online veterinary article I read recently, suggested that research supports the use of the pessoa training aid in the horse's recovery from limb problems, due to its ability to improve posture, and stimulate the core muscles with no undue stress on the legs.

I trust that if you are to consider the use of the pessoa or any other training aid, you will have thorough preparation and knowledge in its correct use and adjustment, and a good eye and foresight. Unfortunately, for the horse, some buyers of gadgets already believe themselves to be experts, and so the human creates yet another piece of artillery!

The bit

The bit is often fitted without any consideration whatsoever for the shape and size of the horse's mouth cavity, many of them fitted in the name of fashion!

Regularly, the type of bit used is based on the theory that **if a top dressage or event rider is using this bit, I must have it too**, without first taking the time to learn why that particular bit is used, how it works, and the effect it has on the inside of the mouth.

I recently read a magazine article in which the writer requested advice on why her horse might be constantly sticking her tongue out to one side when bitted. She was adamant that the bit was not to blame because it was a particular well known training bit! The answer given by a respected equestrian author was probably not the answer the enquirer expected! I hope she took the advice given. I will enlighten you as to why the scenario is a common and neglected event.

Because the bit lies out of sight in the cavity of the mouth, it is often also out of mind. If equestrians took the time to open and scrutinise the horse's mouth, they would see that essentially, there is no room for anything other than his tongue:

■ The tongue lies sandwiched between the top and bottom teeth; it quite visibly cushions the whole area, sometimes even overlapping the surface of the teeth.

■ The bottom part of the interdental space known as the bars lies lower than the surface of the tongue. It is important to remember - although often neglected despite the common use of the phrase **sensitive bars** - the bars are simply bone covered by nerves, blood vessels, and a very thin layer of flesh.

■ Although there may be no visible signs of wolf teeth on the gum surface, sometimes they are present under the sensitive bar tissue, and can be quite painful under pressure.

■ Routinely, we are taught that when bridled, **the bit rests on the sensitive bars**. However, as the tongue's surface invariably sits much higher than the surface of the bars, **clearly, the bit must push down into the surface of the tongue to some extent to make contact with the bars.**

The amount of discomfort and pressure applied by the bit will depend on:

■ The thickness of the tongue.

■ The size of the mouth cavity.

■ The shape of the roof of the mouth.

■ The type and size of the bit used.

Of course, this is only the tip of the iceberg.

FACT: If the corners of the lips, gums, tongue, and roof of the mouth of horses and ponies were as sensitive as those of humans, they probably would not have survived their environment. Nevertheless, they are still exceedingly sensitive to our continuous abusive treatment. Remaining blasé to that fact makes life easier for the human!

At this point, I would like to tell you about my encounter with a special person whilst attending an Equine Reiki Drum course. I noticed she initially had difficulty holding and tapping the drum with her arthritic fingers. She demonstrated how she couldn't make a fist. When riding, she managed to hold her reins only by placing her thumbs over her index fingers.

Elinor, a retired schoolteacher told me that for years, her horse had intermittently snatched the reins and, as the arthritis advanced, she could no longer grip sufficiently to resist the sudden unexpected pull. (The mare was ridden and competed for many years in a copper KK loose ring bradoon snaffle.) She read about the barbaric nature of 'conventional' bits and, after researching bitless bridles, decided to try the Dr Cook Cross-under style.

From the outset of wearing the bridle, the horse settled well and, as a bonus, Elinor noticed that Sophie no longer felt the need to pull! There is no doubt in my mind that their relationship and bond continues to grow.

It is with Elinor's kind permission that I convey her experience, and her quote, *"I don't feel we were ever 'at war' – I just wanted that 'instrument of torture' out of her mouth!"*

Are you yet convinced of the debilitating effects on the horse by **any type of bit?**

Reasons for evasion of the bit

Discomfort in and around the mouth is usually the cause of evasion.

- Primarily, it is because **the horse's mouth was not designed to have a chunk of metal forced in to it.**

- The horse may have a dental problem. Before anything else, the horse's mouth should be checked if he shows any signs of discomfort. Along with the list of signs of evasion given shortly, signs of dental problems may include sensitive cheeks, bad breath, dunking hay in the water, dribbling feed from his mouth, bolting his food, head shaking, tilting his head, crib-biting.

■ The rider has unsteady hands due to her unbalance and tension, or her actions are deliberate, such as seesawing, pulling, or bumping on the horse's mouth. Are you aware that this abuse can also break the horse's teeth or fracture the bones in his mouth, even cause headaches or worse, psychological effects?

■ Extremely serious complications can result from the lack of regular expert dental examinations and procedures, combined with bad handling of the tongue during those processes, such as holding the tongue at an abnormal angle, holding it too tightly, pulling, tying the tongue down, or twitching the horse's ear in an attempt to restrain him. Abusive bits, nosebands and hands can also complicate matters. Every one of these acts has the potential to damage the temporomandibular joint.

■ The bit may be too thick. In an attempt to alleviate the irritation, discomfort, or even pain caused by the bit, the horse will use his tongue in attempt to push the bit out of the way, or he will put his tongue out to the side - if his mouth isn't blocked by the noseband. He may cross his jaw or try to grab the bit with his teeth. He will open his mouth; even flip his tongue over the bit in a bid to prevent the joint of a snaffle bit hitting the roof of his mouth. However, because his tongue is one of the most sensitive organs in his body, the pain will simply spread. If the bit is too thick for his mouth, the horse will be unable to swallow because his tongue will be even more restricted.

- Hold your tongue down with your finger; now try to swallow – impossible isn't it! Have you noticed that as you press down with your finger, your tongue forms an arch at the back, blocking your throat? I am confident the horse will suffer the same experience whenever any kind of bit pressure is placed on his tongue.

■ A bit that is too thin will place more pressure over a smaller area than a thicker bit causing increased discomfort.

■ The bit may be too long, resulting in too much play through the mouth from one side to the other. The joint of the bit may be pulled by the rein from the centre of the mouth to its edge, where it will pinch the margin of the lip and cause soreness. When asked to go in one direction, the horse will attempt to turn in the opposite direction to avoid the pinch.

■ The V shape formed by single jointed bits will not bode well with the shape of the horse's mouth; the joint has the capacity to connect with, and damage the roof of the mouth when in the wrong hands.

■ The bit may be too loose; it will be too far below the crease of the lips, causing the horse to constantly chew and attempt to suck the bit back up to a more comfortable position in the lip corners.

■ The rotational design of a loose ring snaffle can result in soreness of the cheeks from rubbing if the bit is too short in length.

■ The curb chain or strap activated by the curb bit leverage can have differing amounts of thumbscrew action on the jawbone, depending on its tightness.

Despite the Pelham bit being a popular 'solution' for strong, forward pulling horses that are 'hard in the mouth' (yet another term invented by humans as an excuse to place blame on the horse because he has learned to close his mind to our insensitivities), it can have serious detrimental consequences in the wrong hands. Rather than an uninformed decision to fit the horse with a curb bit, the reasons for his behaviour should be fully investigated.

■ Did you know that a 'hard mouth' could also be the result of a back problem due to rider fault, ill-fitting saddle, maybe even a crooked horse? The horse will be reluctant to stretch his neck; his lower neck muscles will over develop. His gait will also be affected.

■ The fitting of the Pelham bit will only serve to contain his symptoms in a punishable way. He will no longer pull or rush; his head will appear to be in an outline and 'on the bit'. He may appear to be comfortable, but in fact, his outline will be the result of force and pressure, and his 'comfortable appearance' will be due to the blocks all around his head, making it impossible for him to object. He will not be 'on the bit'. His head will be unnaturally tucked in, partly due to the force on the rein and also because he will be afraid to touch the bit, which will give the rider a false sense of lightness in her hands.

Whether riding for leisure, event riding or riding a dressage test, you must be constantly aware of the level of pressure placed on the bit through the reins. Riders often tend to hold a firm rein because it 'makes them feel safe'. Only recently, I overheard a top event rider advising other equestrians on how she always likes to keep quite a firm rein as it makes her feel safe! There was no consideration given to the restrictive pressure from the bit, the noseband, the flash, or the resulting blocking through the horse's head.

I was told many years ago that if a rider wants to be the best she can be, she should not compete. As the years have passed, I have developed a deeper understanding of his statement and a growing need to reach out to those of us who still unwittingly abuse our horses in our quest to push them further and further away from their natural being.

■ A bit with a port of any size has the potential to damage the roof of the horse's mouth.

■ The rider is incapable of managing the bit delicately.

■ The use of gadgets.

The measurement of a bit depends on the type of bit required. Don't fall into the trap of believing that once you have the measurement of the horse's mouth, any bit of the same size will fit.

There is no indication in the above list of evasions due to naughtiness by the horse!

Evasion of the bit is not a bad habit, it is self-defence!

I recall uproar some years ago when the horse of a Swedish Olympic rider was constantly ridden with his neck in hyper-flexion (Rollkur). The subsequent excessive restriction on the horse's tongue resulted in a lack of blood supply, causing the tongue to turn blue. The horse pushed his tongue out through the side of his mouth in an attempt to relieve the pressure.

However, because other competitors were riding in the same way, the complaints received by the International Federation for Equestrian Sports from spectators, were not taken seriously. Only when a horse succeeds in pushing his tongue out of his mouth, is the lack of blood supply obvious. I am in trepidation of the number of horses out there who are not able to find that little bit of relief, until his abuser physically removes the bit.

Over extension of the neck is still common practice while uninformed fans look on with admiration. The rollkur debate continues. Rollkur has been redefined; the forced over extension of the head and neck is now considered unacceptable by the FEI. However working a horse low, deep and round (LDR) is acceptable. So, does this mean it is still acceptable for the rider to continue to work the horse with his head **behind** the vertical? The positioning of the horse's head of any depth behind the vertical is bordering on over flexion and abuse.

Continuous, is the mind-set that a certain bit will correct a particular behaviour, such as the use of the Pelham on a horse that pulls. The question **"Why is the horse pulling against the bit"** doesn't arise.

Some horses are merely keen to get on with the job and may get over excited, but that doesn't justify the use of **artillery**. A more severe bit will cause more pain and discomfort. A milder bit together with time, patience, and lots of stimulating schooling is the next best answer to no bit!

Signs of evasion

The following broad list of possible signs of evasion is regularly misinterpreted as misbehaviour. The horse:

- Begins well but becomes more resistant.

- Snatches at the bit.

- Shakes his head.

- Becomes overbent.

- Forces his tongue over the bit or out of the side of his mouth.

- Opens his mouth.

- Crosses his jaw.

- Grinds his teeth.

- Becomes nervous of any rein contact.

- Becomes tight through his poll and jaw.

- Becomes restless.

- Becomes anxious.

- No longer complies.

- Is unwilling to slow or stop.

- Bucks.

- Rears.

- Bolts.

- Naps.

- Prances or rushes when given the aid to slow down or back up.

- Goes into reverse when asked to go forward.

- Appears stiff through his head and neck.

- Becomes over excited when collection is requested.

- Attempts to rub the rider's leg with his head to get her off.

- Becomes clumsy and may stumble.

- Shows no co-ordination in his gait.

- Appears to be lazy.

Bear in mind that the horse is not limited to only one evasion at a time; many of the above come hand in hand. I can assure you that in most cases when ridden without the bit, and where a dental problem is eliminated, the same horse would likely show no signs of **misbehaviour**. The remaining cases are probably also suffering the effects of an ill-fitting saddle!

I am familiar of two proverbs:
No foot, no horse,
and
No mouth, no brakes, no steering.

I have created a much improved 21ˢᵗ century adage:
No bit, no pain, no evasion!

To bit or not to bit – that is the question

This question continues to cause heated debate throughout every media and discussion platform.

There is a variety of reasons out there, of why we consider we should or should not bit a horse based on:

- rules of competition

- our preference

- our confidence levels

- our trust (or lack of trust) in the horse

- our beliefs

If I were to, in my role as a teacher, write down the reasons for and against bitting, they would be based on my knowledge, and my uses of the two; however, I would also feel the need to include my personal beliefs and preferences. With that in mind I will put forward a little information below, based on scientific research conducted by W Robert Cook F.R.C.V.S., PhD., published in 2000.

We recognise that the horse can be at rest and eat, or he can participate in some kind of exercise, whether playing with his friends, having a schooling session or even galloping across country. We don't see him doing both at the same time. It is not possible for him to eat and exercise at the same time. However, having a bit in his mouth forces him to feel the effects of both activities simultaneously.

As soon as a bit is placed in the horse's mouth, his soft palate rises to allow the process of the intake of food. This elevation inhibits his breathing; this in turn can affect his performance. Because the brain thinks the horse has food in his mouth, the production of saliva also begins.

Dr Cook's research shows the detrimental effects of these and many more forced actions and behaviours. You will find the published document simply by searching online for 'A solution to respiratory and other problems caused by the bit' by W Robert Cook F.R.C.V.S., PhD.

The benefits of riding bitless

A bridle of any kind can be detrimental in heavy and unforgiving hands. In considering the use of a bitless bridle, it is essential that advice and training is sought from an expert in this particular field. The positive changes for you and the horse can be astounding. Below are a few examples of the benefits of riding bitless.

■ As described earlier, a horse may not be physically or mentally capable of wearing a bit due to current or past injury to the mouth. The benefit here is that a horse can still be ridden if the horse has a sore mouth.

■ His respiratory system is not impeded.

- Whereas the pressure of the bit is concentrated solely on the sensitive mouth, the bitless bridle offers a more gentle pressure around the whole of the head.

- Communication between horse and rider can be much improved. Rather than the myth that the horse would be uncontrollable without a bit, he would not feel the need to escape the pain and discomfort of an ill-fitting bit.

- The horse has more freedom of movement.

- Regularly, riders let it be known that their horses have suddenly stopped 'misbehaving'.

It is essential that you seek expert help when making the transition from bitted to bitless. Ground work will be required due to the new learning experience needed by both horse and rider. Acceptance of the change is not always instant. The information will, I hope, assist in steering you positively towards making a choice with the best interests of the horse in mind rather than one of belief. There is lots of more in depth expert information available should you wish to delve further.

4

Evasion - Part 2: Our artillery

It is with the best intent that a rider places a saddle on the horse's back, regrettably often based on limited knowledge. The same rider often finds it hard to believe that the saddle and its array of accompaniments can actually be the cause of evasion by the horse, particularly when many of the evasions appear to manifest in front of the rider when in the saddle, rather than underneath her. Nevertheless, wherever the manifestation, the finger points at the horse. Here, the author, in her role as a riding coach, supportively describes and gives simple yet detailed problem solvers that will empower you to make informed choices based on the present fit of your saddle, and to seek help from an expert saddle fitter when appropriate.

Based on what might be limited knowledge, you will do your best to ensure a correctly fitting saddle. You may find it hard to believe that the saddle and its array of accompaniments can actually be the cause of evasion by the horse, particularly when many of the evasions appear to manifest in front of you when in the saddle, rather than underneath you. Nevertheless, wherever the manifestation, you may be tempted to point a finger at the horse.

It is not enough to say that if a saddle is unbalanced it will affect your riding position in a particular way, and the horse will not be able to carry himself properly. It goes much deeper, and as you read on, I am confident you will begin to see with clearer eyes and mind.

Our artillery

The saddle (The Vice)

The art of saddle design, construction, and fitting is fascinating to say the least; it has become a science best left to the experts in this field - the members of the Society of Master Saddlers. A Master Saddler who has also qualified as a saddle fitter should always carry out fitting!

Important news flash –
does your saddle fit you?

Has the thought crossed your mind that your saddle may not fit you, and that you could be the cause of many problems your horse may suffer?

Fitting a saddle to you is **almost** as important as fitting the saddle to the horse, but often, this aspect is neglected.

In the past, I would have riders test the saddle's suitability by completing the hands width test: when sitting in the saddle, the rider should be able to fit comfortably, the width of at least four fingers between the back of her seat and the cantle, and the same between the front of her seat and the pommel. Although it may still act as a general guide, it doesn't give such an exact measurement in today's array of saddles and rider preference.

However, it is essential that the saddle seat is not so large that you constantly slide between the pommel and the cantle, with flaps the size of battle ships, and the loss of your leg aids.

The saddle seat should not be so short that your bottom hangs over the back of the cantle (placing pressure in that area), and the flaps are so small that your knees fall over the edge.

Regrettably, rider preference does sometimes tend to take over the needs and comfort of the horse; in those cases, the saddle should come with a warning sign. The horse's welfare might then be a conscious consideration!

Riding school horses tend to suffer somewhat due to the various sizes of riders they must accommodate, even though the saddle may have been expertly fitted to the horse.

A QUICK CHECKLIST

- The saddle is fit for its purpose.

- The saddle houses your seat comfortably, and you are able to sit in balance.

- The placing of your seat bones allows your weight to naturally balance on the saddle seat, over your feet.

- When standing on the stirrups, your weight naturally balances over your feet, the natural curves in your back act as shock absorbers.

- Leaning forward and sitting back comes easily as your legs remain happily in their natural riding position.

- Your inner thigh is parallel to the front of the flap.

The flap is of appropriate length that it doesn't interfere with your leg connections, and it is not caught up in the top of your boots. Remember that your legs will be at different lengths depending on the discipline you are riding.

- The flap is of adequate width to allow for your legs in jumping position.

- If you are still working on your own balance in the saddle, a correctly fitted saddle will help you in your quest.

- Any deviation from correct balance due to the saddle's unsuitability for you will have severe consequences for you and the horse. You will simply become another **piece of artillery**.

Facts on the saddle

A saddle can be found for every occasion: dressage, eventing, hunting, jumping, western, endurance, polo, side-saddle, the list goes on; however, the main type used in most riding schools - unless the school specialises in particular disciplines - is the general purpose saddle, which is used for school work, hacking, hunting and low level eventing. Sadly, this type of saddle can never completely fulfil the needs of the individual disciplines as those designed specifically; however, it does its job for the lower level riders, as long as the saddle fits the horse and rider correctly.

A saddle designed and fitted by a qualified Master Saddler/ Fitter can be tremendously expensive; I can fully understand why many people drive to the tack shop armed with the length and width measurement of the saddle they want, expecting it to fit the horse.

When looking to buy a new saddle 'off the peg', you must be aware that the saddletree under the leatherwork is usually a standard symmetrical design template for all the saddles of the same type and size on display. Therefore, although the length and width of it may look correct for your horse, the saddle will not fit correctly if he is not also symmetrical on both sides of his body.

Manufactured trees can sometimes be imperfect, throwing the whole balance off, which will have an unfavourable effect on the wellbeing of your horse. The attachments to the warped tree such as the girth straps and stirrup bars will be out of alignment, compromising your position in the saddle. The horse will be unable to move freely and he will feel stiff on one rein. If you continue to use the saddle, the horse's muscles and bones will be traumatised, as will his emotional state.

Horses don't know that the saddle is supposed to fit, or that having a rider on board is supposed to be comfortable. He simply works and moves as best he can, often in discomfort and pain. Horses will suffer outright pain, in silence, for years.

Many equestrians are of the opinion that because the horse obeys a command, there is obviously no problem with the fit of the saddle. Any resistance by the horse is misinterpreted as an **attitude** problem; "*He's evading the bit again*" or "*This horse is very lazy*".

An introduction to the saddle for the first time often comes with the clear indication that the horse must never complain about his anxiety or discomfort. It is only the braver horses who dare argue their point!

The saddle fits correctly if you can fit three fingers between the withers and the pommel of the saddle is a very popular phrase, with the added **And you are able to see daylight through the full length of the gullet**, with no indication as to whether the fingers are those of large burly adults or small children! However, it has always been a basic guide and has worked minimally I suppose.

Nowadays, the space under the pommel bears very little relevance to the correct fitting of a saddle. The clearance between the pommel and the wither depends on the type of saddle; for example, there will be much less clearance on a close contact or flat seat saddle such as a jumping saddle, than with other types such as the general purpose saddle and the deeper seat saddles. However, if the clearance is higher than three inches, then it would more than likely indicate that the tree is too narrow.

The adequate clearance along the whole length of the gullet, both **without** and **with** the rider on-board is what counts.

If you intend putting some kind of saddlecloth underneath, it **must** be taken into account in assessing the gullet space. Don't fall into the trap of having a saddle fitted, then putting a luscious thick sheepskin numnah underneath as an afterthought; it **won't** work!

The actual fitting of the saddle is only a part of the equation. Equally, there should be:

A good farrier: the slightest unevenness of the horse's feet can cause the same along his body, making correct saddle fitting difficult. Uneven feet are not always down to the actions of the farrier. One-sidedness of the horse is a common cause of irregularities of the feet, due to irregular weight on each front leg.

Balanced nutrition and good training of the horse: to assist in the correct building of weight, muscle, strength and top line that is necessary for correct, comfortable saddle fitting.

Effective management: a horse's back can change shape according to his health, management, growth, work and even the season, which will have a direct influence on the fit and comfort of the saddle on his back.

The horse's weight

If you don't know the weight of your horse, how can you ensure his wellbeing? He will begin to suffer an element of discomfort under saddle the moment he begins to gain weight. However, the visible signs may not be apparent for some time.

How often have you fastened the girth with the thought that it felt a little tighter than the last time, or that the horse was blowing himself out; but you then let the thought pass and fastened the girth up anyway? Was the girth feeling even more snug as you began to run out of girth holes? Did you then spend money on a new girth?

During that time, did you begin to notice any changes in your horse's mood, behaviour, or body language? Maybe he was suffering in silence because he knew his place as his saddle became more debilitating!

The horse will suffer the same kind of discomfort from a saddle that becomes too wide due to weight and muscle loss.

How to weigh your horse

The easiest way to weigh your horse is with a weigh tape, of which you should be familiar. The numbers along its length correspond to the horse's weight in kilos.

- Measuring your horse's weight should be become a natural part of your monthly routine.

- Have some-one hold the horse or tie him up.

- Place the tape around his body about two inches behind his shoulder. If the horse has high withers and the tape slides down, place it a little further back where it will sit more securely.

- If you need to place the tape further back, make sure you measure from the same place every time, otherwise discrepancies will arise in the measurement readings.

- Hold the tape firm enough so that it makes a slight indent in the hair.

- Record every weight measurement to enable positive all round management decisions in the correct saddle fit for your horse.

The saddle support system

Considering that the horse was not intended to be ridden, have you ever stopped to consider what goes on underneath the saddle as you place it on the horse's back, or the effect the saddle may have on the horse's anatomy as a whole? An ill-fitting saddle can have a devastating impact on his entire being.

- The saddle sits over the longissimus dorsi, latissimus dorsi and the thoracic part of the trapezius muscle. The pressure of an ill-fitting saddle will cause the muscles to contract, resulting in pain. The point of the stirrup bar can be potential artillery when aimed at the shoulder.

- Soft tissue damage to the longissimus dorsi - the main muscle that supports the back and stabilises the spine with the front part lying underneath the shoulder blade - will result in the horse being unable to achieve a correct outline; his back will hollow as he raises his head. He will try to compensate by using his body differently and less effectively, resulting in possible behavioural issues and lameness due to excess strain on his joints.

- The restricted latissimus dorsi will be unable to complete its task of supporting the horse's back, flexing his shoulder, and pulling the foreleg back.

- The thoracic trapezius stems from the supraspinous ligament; it lies over the shoulder blade and sits underneath the saddle gullet. A restrictive saddle will prevent this muscle from pulling the shoulder blade backward and upward.

- The restricted cervical trapezius, which originates in the nuchal ligament and sits in front of the saddle, will be denied the role of pulling the shoulder blade forward and upward as it contracts and shortens. The result will be a short choppy stride.

- Wastage of this part of the muscle will become evident by the eventual dip in front of the withers.

■ A strong thick layer of connective tissue called the lumbodorsal fascia that helps to protect these muscles subsequently receives a fair amount of abuse.

■ The pain will cause the horse to avoid using these muscles, resulting in musculoskeletal imbalances.

■ In the middle of the triangle formed by the latter part of the trapezius muscle and the back of the shoulder, sits a cranial nerve, commonly known as the accessory nerve or CN11. The slightest pressure on the nerve will have a reflex action:

   - The horse will not go forward.

   - He will twitch his withers and hollow through his spine.

   - He will not be able to use his abdominal muscles due to the hollowness through his back.

   - He will not be able to engage his hindquarters or carry out any movement.

   - His distress will be more apparent as he pins his ears back.

   - Shortened choppy strides can cause the posterior pectoral muscle that lies just behind the horse's front leg in the girth area, to stiffen, and inhibit its ability to contract and pull the front leg back. Because it is then unable to relax and release the flow of the leg, its opposite muscle will have difficulty in serving the forward movement of the leg.

   - Because the front and hind legs are built to work in unison, the movement of the hindquarters will be affected.

■ As the longissimus dorsi, psoas and gluteal muscles develop, the saddle will sit differently at the cantle, changing your position in the saddle. The neglect of correct saddle fit due to any type of muscle changes, will adversely change your position in the saddle and the performance of the horse.

■ Misfiring muscles anywhere in the horse's body will have the effect of the tremors of an earthquake ricocheting out from the source, affecting his complete physical and emotional wellbeing.

■ Muscles must work in pairs; when one is compromised, it will adversely affect its opposite.

■ Compromise of the muscles will result in a skeleton that is unable to perform correctly.

■ Watch out for signs of wastage of the trapezius, latissimus dorsi, and spinalis dorsi due to an ill-fitting saddle or ineffective riding.

■ White hairs are a good tell-tale sign of pressure points. Unfortunately, they are not the first signs! They appear over time when the constant pressure has damaged the hair follicles and skin tissue.

In the interests of your safety, I suggest you listen to the subtle hints of his distaste!

The fitting of the saddle, farriery, nutrition, and good training are only half of the job; the other half is watching the horse work, particularly in a circle, to ensure there is no movement in the saddle. If you watch and listen to the horse during this process, he will tell you if the saddle is, or is **not**, comfortable.

Unlike humans, horses don't express their pain clearly; they tend to hide it from us or give the subtlest of hints. Unfortunately, when the pain gets so bad that they begin to shout it from the rooftops, the damage is already done.

Make sure you take notice of him every step of the way, because it may have serious repercussions if you don't!

Fitting a correctly balanced saddle, and ensuring the stirrup bar and girth are suitably placed to horses of differing shapes, sizes and lop-sidedness, can be difficult.

However, many saddles now come with additions to accommodate the horse as he changes shape due to growth, work, health, diet, and so on.

Numerous saddles also take into account the needs of the rider, including adjustable stirrup bars, seat adjustments, and adjustable knee rolls.

Saddles are also available with an adjustable three-position flap to accommodate the disciplines of dressage, jumping and general purpose, and cross-country, all in one saddle.

The treeless saddles are popular nowadays because they adapt to asymmetrical horses and those with high withers and wide backs; they are designed for optimum comfort for both horse and rider. Correct fitting is essential.

The rider has a much closer contact through her body than with traditional treed saddles. Some say that there must be an element of rider balance and a quiet seat due to the close contact of horse and rider. Others are of the opinion that the closeness improves the novice rider's ability to feel the rhythm of the horse, resulting in her achieving balance much quicker. It appears to me then, that even the treeless saddle may be **detrimental** in the wrong hands. If the novice can easily feel the movement of the horse, imagine what he can feel on his back.

Saddle fitting simplified to prevent further attack and friendly fire!

The following guidance is simply to help you take steps in determining the source of a particular problem. If the source lies with the saddle, you should not subject your horse to any further misery.

My role as a **teacher** is to provide you with awareness in the essentials of the on-going good fit of your **existing** saddle to both you and your horse, through simple processes that will help you to eradicate problems occurring due to an ill fit, and empower you to **seek expert assistance when problems are uncovered with the saddle.**

Guidance from a Master Saddler/Fitter can be instrumental in yours and your horse's future success and wellbeing. The details for Master Saddlers/Fitters local to you can be found on the Society of Master Saddlers' website.

Most of our **artillery**, of which the treed saddle plays a vital part, backfires at our attempts to attack the horse, because we simply don't realise that we are our own enemy.

Liberate yourself from the mind-set that a saddle expertly fitted to both you and your horse will remain a perfect fit; you must ensure the saddle continues to suit both of you to guarantee the ultimate wellbeing and performance of you and the horse.

The recommended professional saddle check interval is at least every three to six months, depending on the changes that occur. Stick to all the considerations listed earlier.

Between the ages of 4 and 7, many changes can occur in the horse's shape as he grows. I am not an advocate of backing a horse while his spine is still being 'modelled'. However, I place importance on light groundwork and play as soon as possible, to stimulate and strengthen the bones and cartilage, muscles, tendons and ligaments in readiness for his working career.

A growing rider also goes through many changes, all of which will affect the way the saddle sits on the horse. These too must be carefully measured.

★   ★   ★

How often do you actually look at, and touch your horse with your hands, I mean **REALLY** look into his eyes, caress him with feeling over his head, eyes, ears, muzzle, neck, body, legs, and tail? Not only will he appreciate the calming influence of your hands and your slow deep breath, done regularly, you will get to know every part of him: his lumps, bumps and blemishes; you will begin to recognise quickly when something is amiss. If your horse isn't used to being touched in this way, begin slowly while gaining his trust.

Regular checking by you of the horse's back for soreness is necessary. Below is a simple, yet effective test in detecting the slightest discomfort the horse might be suffering. It takes no more than five minutes. Try to fit a session into your daily routine; you owe it to your horse.

His reactions will indicate immediately if there is a problem in the area manipulated that needs expert treatment. Look out for any reaction, which may range from a subtle swish of the tail to a hollowing of the back, to the horse turning his head to bite you.

If you are inexperienced and lack knowledge of the horse's anatomy and the saddle, you should not attempt to manipulate your horse in any way, or attempt to check the fit a saddle without expert supervision.

- Have someone hold the horse steady for you.

- Ensure he is standing square. He may find this difficult if he is not symmetrical.

To start on the left hand side of the horse:

- Cup the fingers of your right hand over the spine so that the tips of your fingers feel the edge of the spine on the right hand side. With a little pressure, run your fingers along the length of the spine.

- Press the tips of your fingers down on, and around the whole sacral area. He will dip if there is any discomfort in that area.

- Rake the fingers of one hand down the left trapezius muscle.

- Carry on from the trapezius muscle, along the latissimus and longissimus dorsi muscles to the lumbar region. He will dip his back if he feels discomfort.

- Change sides and repeat the process.

Once you have completed the above examination, with your horse's permission, give him a well-deserved gentle massage.

Don't be afraid to run the flat of your hand and fingers against his muscles. You simply apply the same principle as if you were massaging your own muscles when they feel tired and sore, or cramping.

You don't need to put all your strength behind your manipulation, as a professional would do; just a gentle pressure as if kneading dough will relax your horse. We all enjoy a massage after a hard physical or stressful day.

A relaxed muscle will feel soft and flat. If sore or cramping, it will feel tight and knotted. If the latter, your horse may object to your handling of him; be alert.

Massage, followed by exercise helps to kick-start the muscles. When my body has had a massage, I naturally feel the need to stretch my muscles. It is necessary for the horse too.

However, whereas I am satisfied with a brisk walk with my dogs, canter work for the horse is ideal for muscle lengthening and loosening on completion of a correct warm up, providing you have found no problems during your checks.

Below are a few possible areas of concern that may help you in your inspection described above.

■ Pain in the sacroiliac area could be due to a damaged joint or the muscles and ligaments around the joint. It is also possible that the horse is trying to compensate for pain elsewhere.

■ Any soreness in the lumbar region of an asymmetrical horse may originate from the loaded shoulder colliding with the front of the saddle as the shoulder rotates during movement. The collision will push the saddle back causing it to slide, rub, and cause soreness at that point.

■ A croup high horse will also often suffer problems around the lumbar region as well as the withers because of an ill-fitting saddle. Of course, the saddle is not always the culprit.

■ Injuries from falls and knocks, and hereditary or degenerative problems of any kind, can have a physical, behavioural, and emotional impact on the horse.

If the horse gives any indication of discomfort, no matter how vague, don't attempt to put on the saddle. You must seek expert advice.

On confirmation that the horse has a clean bill of health, you should make every effort to ensure the saddle fits the horse correctly.

It is **not** good for the horse for you to saddle him up and then jump on his back in order to check if the saddle fits! Below is a stripped down to the bare basics, step-by-step guide in the regular checking of the fit of your existing saddle, together with problems arising due to an incorrect fit.

The instructions given in **Phases 1 and 2** of the guide will help to eliminate the needless discomfort of the horse.

The complete guide will empower you in making better-informed choices and actions.

The saddle fitting problems listed are by no means exhaustive; however, they will go some way in unlocking the key to your mind and helping you to think outside of the box.

If you recognise that your current saddle is in disagreement with your horse, you must seek expert advice.

Stand the horse square on a flat surface.

Phase 1 – Don't pick up the saddle yet!
Shoulder blade rotation measurement

A vital first step in ensuring the correct saddle fit is being aware of the rotational capability of each scapula (shoulder blade). When in place, the opening of the saddle gullet must allow sufficient clearance especially at the sides, to accommodate without hindrance, the tremendous range of upward and backward motion of the cartilage-topped scapula towards the opening of the gullet.

The points of the saddle must not sit further forward than the back of the scapula and the muscles covering the area.

CHECKLIST

- Feel where the back of the horse's scapula is at rest; mark it with chalk.

- Pick up his leg behind the knee and gently extend it forward. Don't attempt to straighten his leg because his tendons would be at risk.

- His scapula will rotate back; the distance will depend on how upright or sloping the shoulder is. If the scapula is difficult to find when the horse is still, have some-one lead him while you walk along with your hand on his shoulder; you will feel the scapula rotate along its route as the horse moves forwards.

- Mark the spot of maximum rotation with the chalk, then measure the distance between the two. The horse's shoulders must be free to rotate the full distance of the measurement when the saddle is on his back; as the horse moves his foreleg **forward**, the top of the scapula moves **backward** and the muscle bulges.

Spinal width measurement

The correct spine measurement is crucial. It expands out much further than the bony prominences along the middle of the horse's back. There is no scope for approximating here!

CHECKLIST

■ Standing beside and facing the horse, place your fingertips parallel to the spinous processes just to the back of the withers, in the area where the saddle sits.

■ Rake your fingertips vertically and quite firmly until you feel an indent where the spine ends and the longissimus dorsi muscle can be felt.

■ Mark the indent with chalk.

■ Repeat the process on the other side of the horse.

■ Place the thumb and index finger of the hand nearest the horse's head on the two chalk marks, to form a bridge over the spine.

■ The four fingers of your free hand should slide easily between the bridge of your opposite hand and the horse's spine; it will determine the correct measurement of the saddle gullet width.

■ Take notice of any gaps between the bridge and your free hand: could you fit another finger in the gap?

■ Do the walls of the bridge block the knuckles of your index finger and little finger? These anomalies must mirror the measurement of your hand against the saddle gullet.

Finding the last rib

The lumbar vertebrae don't afford the same support as the thoracic vertebrae, which have the added stability of the rib cage. It is crucial that the saddle does **not** sit beyond the last vertebrae, as to do so would result in a sore, weakened back.

CHECKLIST

- ■ Run your hands along the ribcage until you touch the last rib.

- ■ Trace the rib upwards towards the spine where it attaches to the vertebra. You will find the track to be a slightly curved angle.

- ■ Mark the area with chalk.

- ■ The area behind the last rib will feel a little bouncy compared to the area in front of it due to its lack of support.

- ■ You now have a visible guide in fitting the saddle in the correct place.

Phase 2 – Now pick up the saddle

Saddletree inspection

The beautiful top layer and the underlying stuffing of the saddle is only as good as the tree it conceals. When did you last check your saddletree for deficiencies?

Turn the saddle face up to expose the gullet

CHECKLIST

- ■ Supporting the gullet over your thigh, place one hand firmly on the twist (waist) of the saddle.

- ■ Take hold of the cantle with your other hand and pull it towards you. A healthy spring tree saddle won't give to the pull, it will flex very slightly, but no more than that. A broken tree will give to the pull. You may even hear it creak.

- Place the saddle upside down on a protective cloth, or turn the saddle around so that the cantle now rests on your thigh.

- Run your eyes along the length of the gullet, drawing an imaginary straight line from the gullet entrance to the centre of the cantle. Any deviation from the straight line will suggest a broken tree.

- Take hold of the sides of the gullet opening; push and pull each side towards and away from the other, listening for any creaks and watching for any movement. The tree extends only part way down the knee roll length, so there will be natural flexibility below it.

Don't use a saddle with a broken tree.

The twist of the saddle

When deciding whether we need a saddle with a narrow twist or a wide twist we very often take into consideration only our own comfort. The twist is the narrowest part of the saddle seat; its where the saddle changes shape (twists) from an angled position where it accommodates the horse's shoulder, to a flat surface.

Ideally, the twist of the saddle will accommodate the twist(s) of the horse. If the saddle is 'off the peg', the twist will be standard based on the template used.

Watch the video 'Understanding the twist of the horse's back', by Carmi Weininger – https://vimeo.com/70523941. The video shows clearly how the angle of the horse's back can change dramatically.

The saddletree angle

If only we had x-ray vision so that we could see underneath all the padding. Would it be helpful to you if you could; would you know what you were looking for? I suggest that all potential buyers of treed saddles should attend a compulsory master class pertaining to the **saddletree**.

I am aware that many people place the most importance on the width and angle of the tree points. However, problems are assured if the bearing surface of the whole tree doesn't match the full bearing surface of the horse.

Think about it, the horse's rib cage is the main enabler of the saddle and rider support, and, as horses and their rib cages come in many different shapes and sizes, it must be a consideration in the manufacture of the tree.

The analysis of the horse's framework from where the front of the saddle sits to his croup will pick up any deviation that requires attention when making the saddle. It is not enough to make one size of a tree with various widths.

Having said that, it doesn't take away the significance of the angle of the tree at its lowest point - the end of the bar that gives strength to the gullet arch and determines the tree width. The bar must be at an angle that allows the horse full freedom of the scapula and its surrounding tissue when in motion. The angle of the tree dictates the fit of the gullet and its panels.

Which would you prefer: to pay for a saddle off the peg and trust that it will fit your horse, or have one made to measure for the trusted comfort of both of you, taking into account that the fit to your horse must take priority over your needs?

What might appear to be expensive at the beginning could potentially turn out to be the best investment you have ever made.

How to check if the angle of the saddletree matches the angle of the horse's shoulder

The simple process below will confirm if the angle of your existing saddle matches the angle of your horse's shoulder. The visual results may shock you!

■ Bendable wire will do the job, but ideally a sixty-centimetre length flexi curve ruler that you can buy from office suppliers or online reasonably cheap, will mould to the horse better.

■ Ask someone to hold the horse, or tie him up.

■ Make sure the saddle is to hand.

■ Lay the flexi curve ruler about two inches behind the horse's scapula in the place where the saddle gullet will sit.

■ Run your hands down each side so that it moulds along its length and over the wither area to the contours of the horse.

■ Remove the flexi curve ruler carefully and sit it at the saddle gullet.

■ Line up one side of the flexi curve ruler with the angle of the saddletree. The other side should also symmetrically line up. However, if it **doesn't** match, your horse will be subjected to pain and discomfort.

The saddle gullet measurement

The gullet must be adequately wide and deep so that the spine remains free of all pressure to avert bruising of the bones and damage of their spinous processes.

CHECKLIST

■ Run the width of your hand along the length of the gullet. The measurement should match that of the measurement you took of the horse's spine width.

The narrow gullet

- If the walls of the saddle gullet entrance block your measured hand width, the saddle is too narrow. The pommel will sit higher than the cantle.

Problems arising if you attempt to ride in this saddle:

- A saddle that is too high at the front and low at the back will force all the combined weight of you and the saddle over the last two floating ribs of the horse.

- He will find it difficult to lift his back.

- Due to the sensation of falling backwards, your knees may move forwards and your lower legs will then move backwards from the correct position. You may then feel the need to bring your torso forward, sit over your legs, and roll your shoulders forward in attempt to re-balance yourself.

- Even if the width of the gullet entrance fits well, the saddle is too narrow for your horse's back if the gullet tapers along its length and becomes too narrow to accommodate your measured hand width.

- The saddle, along with the saddle points may sit tight and flush behind the chalked shoulder measurement at rest; the scapula will be unable to travel backwards as the horse moves his front leg forwards. (The saddle points are the end of the inverted U shaped arch that points downward on to the tree, and are the lowest parts of the saddle tree to rest on the horse).

- The pinching and blocking of the saddle and the points against the shoulder will cause the horse to take short choppy strides. He will become touchy and irritable.

- Because the saddle tips backwards, it will create pressure on the loins forcing the horse to leave his quarters behind, placing strain on the hock and stifle with resulting pain.

- The saddle is in danger of sitting too close to the spine, pinching and damaging the wither muscles and rubbing the ligament. It will also cause the horse to tighten his muscles and hollow his back, causing long-term damage. The horse will drop his back to avoid using his wither muscles. Due to a lack of use, the muscles will waste away.

- The constant pressure on and around the withers or any other part of the horse's back will impair the circulation which can make the hair turn white, a process known as necrosis.

- When moving in a circle and around a corner, the horse bends his body within his spinal limits to match the curvature of the shape he is travelling. The unyielding gullet of the saddle is unable to mirror the same arc; the saddle, subsequently displaced to the outside, will cause the panel on the inside of the circle to cross over and sit on the spine.

- The horse's back will hollow as he tightens the muscles.

- Consistent use of this saddle will cause severe injury with likely irreversible damage to the spine. Meanwhile, his signs of pain will become more frequent and more volatile as he begins to bolt, buck, rear, bite, and so on!

The wide gullet

- If the gullet measurement is wider than the measurement of the spine width, the saddle is too wide for the horse's back.

- The underside of the pommel arch may bear down on the withers, while the sides of the gullet bear down on the shoulder muscles.

Problems arising if you attempt to ride in this saddle:

- The panels will sit too low over the spine, drastically reducing their protective function to the point where they can no longer support and efficiently distribute your weight.

- The pressure of the saddle being too high at the back and low in front will travel forward to the horse's shoulders, causing pinching of the sides of the withers.

- The knock on effect of pressure points under the saddle area will result in possible long-term damage to the withers, spine, and muscles. Necrosis can be a problem here too.

- Because the saddle sits too low at the front, you may be thrown forward onto a fork seat, drastically increasing the pressure at the front of the saddle.

- Your lower back will suffer detriment as you lean back to compensate for the forward force of your torso. To lighten the discomfort of your lower back, you may lift your legs up into a chair seat, a very uncomfortable position for both of you.

Both scenarios will make it extremely difficult for you and the horse to balance correctly when you are in the saddle.

If the saddle has passed the gullet measurement test, move on to checking the saddle panels.

Scrutinise the saddle panels

The panels are a very important component of the saddle. Any problems here and your horse will know about it. However, will you?

They are the shock absorbers; they act as a buffer for your seat. They also protect the horse from the impact of both you and the saddle, by evenly distributing the combined weight away from the sensitive spinous area of the withers and spine. It is crucial that the panels remain in tiptop condition.

The shape of your horse's back will differ from another horse; one horse may have a flat back, another may be round. If the shape of the tree doesn't match your horse, the focus of your body weight may be on the edges of the panels, causing painful pressure points.

CHECKLIST

- Thoroughly run the flat of your fingers along the panels, feeling for the slightest bump or depression. The slightest imperfection can have a drastic effect on the movement and wellbeing of your horse.

- The appearance of dimples in the area below where your seat bones rest is a sure sign that attention is needed.

- If the panels look and feel deflated, or the two panels appear to differ in shape, re-stuffing is necessary.

- Panels fitted with airbags rather than stuffing will need adjustment or special maintenance by a saddler, only as the horse changes shape.

- Uneven or insufficient stuffing will be apparent by the appearance of uneven shedding of the horse's seasonal coat under the saddle area, as well as possible clumps of hair dotted around the panel.

- Look for any loose threads around the stitching. Bear in mind that saddle makers leave part of the stitching incomplete for easy access when re-stuffing is needed.

- Wear and tear can compress the stuffing over a short period, sufficiently reducing the panel thickness to cause behavioural signs in your horse.

Problems arising if you attempt to ride in a saddle with imperfections

- Pressure points caused by uneven flocking can cause hair loss and a reduction of blood flow to the area.

- Back problems may be the result of pressure points.

- Any unevenness in your riding position will cause the same in the stuffing.

- If you always mount from the left side, the left panel will flatten.

- If you are lopsided, however slight, the panels will become lopsided.

- Your lopsidedness will affect the horse's balance; he will become uneven.

- Lopsided muscles cause pain, stiffness, and restriction of movement. The horse will be prone to sprains and other injuries.

- Other causes of injury are noticeable once the saddle is on the horse's back; they are explained below in **'Effective panel contact'**.

Phase 3 - Ready for fitting

Only when Phases 1 and 2 share a positive outcome, is the saddle placed on the horse's back.

Correct saddle length

If the relevant measurements already taken of both horse and saddle are correct, the saddle will sit comfortably.

CHECKLIST

- Minus all the accessories, place the saddle just above the withers; slide it back until it 'naturally falls into place' behind the shoulder blades where the mane ends.

- The length of the saddle should fit between the chalk lines at the back of the shoulder and the last rib, allowing for the correct positioning of the saddle points.

- Do **not** slide the saddle towards the withers once it has connected with the horse's back. Have you ever suffered from a sore head because your hair was forced against its natural lay? Then spare a thought for the horse.

- If the saddle sits beyond the chalk mark at the last rib, don't attempt to fit this saddle.

Problems arising if you attempt to ride in a saddle that is too long:

- The back of the saddle will sit on the weak lumbar area, unsupported. The horse's kidneys are housed in this area.

- The soreness will cause the horse to react in many ways such as avoiding you when you approach him, saddle in hand, or dipping his back when the saddle makes contact with his back.

- As you mount up, he may try to run away from the saddle above him.

- As the pain worsens he may buck in an attempt to rid himself of the weight; this may only serve to push the saddle forwards onto the shoulder, resulting in likely damage to the cartilage and bone of the scapula.

The correctly balanced saddle

A correctly balanced saddle will place your seat properly and distribute your weight over a large area of the saddle seat, without undue pressure on the horse's shoulders or hindquarters.

If your previous measurements are rock-solid and you are confident of no asymmetrical issues that affect the fit of the saddle, the following pencil test will keenly confirm that the saddle is balanced accurately.

CHECKLIST

- The cantle should be higher than the pommel, the height is usually minimal in flat seat saddles; the middle of the seat must be the deepest part and parallel to the floor.

■ Place a pencil or piece of chalk in the centre of the saddle seat. The object will remain static if the seat is level.

■ It will roll forward towards the pommel if the saddle sits lower at the front than at the back. The cause is usually too wide a pommel.

■ It will roll towards the cantle if the saddle is higher at the front than at the back. The causes may be that the horse has excessively high withers or the saddle gullet is too narrow.

Any lop-sidedness, be it due to conformation, fatty tissue or an already ill-fitting saddle, will become apparent as soon as the saddle makes contact with the horse's back.

■ Looking from behind the horse, the middle of the cantle will be off centre of the spine as the larger of the shoulder muscles pushes the saddle out and back, causing the top of the panel and the point of the tree on the opposite side to press down over the shoulder. Bear in mind the saddle is sitting without the addition of a fastened girth.

■ The panel on the loaded shoulder side may be dangerously close to the spine.

■ The panel on the side of the larger muscle may sit higher along its length than its opposite.

Are you beginning to see the bigger picture?

Problems arising if you attempt to ride in this saddle

■ The fastened girth will ensure the added pressure of the points bearing down. The horse will no longer have the light relief of the panel on the loaded shoulder side being shifted out and back slightly; the saddle will now be pinned down. No matter how the horse tries to evade the pain, the girth will make sure it stays with him.

- Every forward movement of his leg on that side will result in the scapula colliding with the saddle panel as the scapula rotates back, causing damage to the saddle support system with a ricocheting effect to both ends of the spectrum. The effect will increase at the canter as the croup pushes the saddle forward with more thrust.

- His whole gait will feel uneven.

- There will be a rolling effect as the saddle is forced from its correct position.

- Your lower back will twist; the horse will suffer detriment to his lumbar-sacral area.

Saddle straightness

When looking from behind the horse, his straight spine should be directly below the centre of the back of the cantle.

Gullet width

It is vital that the gullet has no contact with the horse's spine. It must be sufficiently wide at the back to avoid contact with the spine during turns and circles when the horse's back curves slightly.

There must be ample room under the roof of the gullet opening to accommodate the withers, and the same to allow the smooth movement of the shoulder.

If your previous measurements of the horse's spine and the saddle gullet capacity matched, the gullet should cosset the spine.

CHECKLIST

- Stand to the front of the shoulder and lift up the flap; you will see a small leather pocket in which sits the point of the tree – the end of the front of the saddletree. A metal **gullet plate** attaches to and spans the bridge formed by the front of the gullet. The size of the gullet plate determines the downward angle of each point at the shoulder. The angle of the piping around the front edge of the panels will also give you a clue as to its angle.

■ Run your hand down very slowly from the top of the gullet plate to the **point** located at the bottom. If you feel more pressure at the **point**, with a gap at the top, **the saddle is too narrow**.

■ If you feel more pressure at the top than at the **point**, **the saddle is too wide.**

■ The gullet length follows the straightness of the horse's spine, with daylight passing through. Look, and feel along the space from the front and the back.

If the gullet threatens the horse's spine, however slight, abandon the process.

Please refer to Phase 2 – Saddle gullet measurement - Problems arising if you attempt to ride in this saddle.

Effective panel contact

There must be full panel contact with the horse's back, with even pressure all around to withstand your weight in the saddle. However, his back will change shape as soon as he begins to move.

Modern saddles are still quite rigid; yet the horse must move and alter his shape as he bends his ribcage or arches his back so he can comfortably take your weight, and when he feels the need to hollow his back.

Bridging and Rocking

The above faults occur when the shape of the saddle at any point doesn't match the shape of the horse's back. Rather than resting on the thoracic part of the spine and supporting your weight evenly across the ribcage, it sits over the top of the horse's back like a rod, forming a bridge between the withers and the point at which the panels make contact when you are in the saddle.

The limited contact of the two areas of the saddle at the withers and of those further along will leave the saddle free to move about, rubbing the withers and the horse's back; he will be subjected to insurmountable pressure on these areas resulting in pain, soreness, and even open wounds if prolonged.

CHECKLIST

■ Ensure the front of the saddle clicks into its correct place behind the shoulder.

■ Press down on the saddle seat with one hand while running the other hand between the panel and the horse, feeling for an even contact throughout.

■ The previous checks should have confirmed that the saddle is fit for its purpose. However, if you feel any tight spots, this could indicate that the saddle is too narrow. An indication of the saddle being too wide is if it rests on the withers or rocks front to back.

■ If the full length of the panel doesn't rest evenly on the horse's back (bridging), the saddle will rock. The gap between the horse's back and the panel will be evident as you stand to the side and look. You may even be able to run your hand too easily under the panels. The gap may appear more prominent when the girth is fastened.

■ Push the saddle down with your hand until the gap closes then let it go. It will immediately spring back into its former position if it doesn't fit.

Problems arising if you ride in this saddle:

■ When in walk, pressure will be placed on the four points as given above, resulting in the said injuries.

■ As you rise off the saddle when in trot, the saddle will follow your seat. As you sit down, the panel will also sit on the horse's back with a thud.

■ The horse will become disengaged as he drops his back and stiffens through the longissimus dorsi muscle.

■ Don't be surprised when your horse takes evasive action!

The saddle attachments

Placing of the stirrup bars

How many times has your coach repeated the words *"Keep your legs underneath your body, so that if I whipped the horse away from under you, you would land on your feet and not on your bottom"*? I could very easily have been that coach, knowing only too well that it was nigh on impossible for the rider to keep her legs underneath her because the stirrup bar was sitting too far forward in relation to her seat in the saddle, causing a chair seat and the impairment that came with it.

Eventually I gave up the ghost and taught most of my riders without the hindrance of their stirrups; all were the better for it, not to mention the relief of the horses involved!

Times have changed and saddles now come with adjustable stirrup bars that take into account the required positioning of a rider's leg. The placing of the stirrup bar depends on factors such as the length of your legs, or the type of riding in which you participate.

However, many saddles with the original forward stirrup bars are still in use, causing problems for horse and rider. If you are the owner of this type of saddle, you may have the following problems:

■ The leather doesn't hang vertically.

■ You struggle to maintain an ear, shoulder, hip, heel line, and you are forced into a **chair seat**.

■ Your loss of balance causes the same in the horse with the roll on effect of discomfort and possible injury to the horse's back, and his overall wellbeing.

The ideal of leaving the stirrup bar in the open position so that the stirrup leather could slide away from the bar when a rider falls off and is in danger of being dragged, has always been somewhat controversial. This is particularly so in competitive sports such as show jumping and eventing, when the rider's foot sometimes forces the stirrup and its leather forward, only for it to release itself from the bar at an awkward moment.

In my opinion, the stirrup bars, when used by young, beginner, novice, and general riders, should remain open at all times. Stirrup bars are now often designed to stay open.

Sports competitors will always make their own safety conscious decisions.

Positioning of the girth

The resting position of the fastened girth, both in the horse's static and dynamic conformation, can affect the whole position of the saddle and the horse's performance; yet very little emphasis is placed on its importance.

It is taken for granted that the girth always fits in the horse's girth groove. Although it is normal for the girth groove to be just behind the forearm, it can, on some horses, be found further forward under the forearm, while other horses don't appear to have a groove at all; in fact, the girth of some horses actually bulges. These factors alone make the girth fitting process difficult.

However, we also take it for granted that once the saddle is in its correct place - leaving some space between it and the horse's foreleg – the girth straps are obviously also hanging perfectly for the attachment of the girth.

- Ideally, when fastened, the girth should influence the centre of the saddle, encouraging it to lie flat against the horse, while it also runs perpendicular to the saddle. If the girth groove is within that vertical line too, then life is wonderful. Unfortunately, the vertical fall of the girth straps doesn't always align with the girth groove.

- What may appear to be the ideal spot for the girth to sit when the horse is motionless, can turn out to be quite precarious when he is, for example, in flight over a jump, when his whole body becomes more streamlined as he stretches. If the area of his barrel behind the girth tapers off, the girth may be inclined to follow that direction. The ensuing backward movement of the saddle will compromise the horse and you.

- If his ribcage bulges behind the girth and tapers in front of it, the girth will inch its way forward to settle in its space, pulling the saddle headfirst towards the horse's shoulder. The restriction to the scapula will have the roll on effect I discussed earlier.

- The girth will always naturally move and come to rest at the narrowest part of the horse's torso.

- If the saddle is positioned too far forward, the girth will also sit too far forward, again with detrimental effects.

- The girth will always sit in the position it finds the most appealing, depending on the horse's conformation.

However, the girth usually sits in the area of the pectoral muscles that are prone to soreness and spasm if restricted by the girth.

- A narrow girth will concentrate more pressure in a smaller area, intensifying any pain.

- A wider girth will be more comfortable; it will spread the pressure more evenly.

- A girth with elastic at one end will allow some give without undue saddle movement. Fasten and tighten the girth equally at each side so that the load is equally shared.

- The girth's tightest spot is always under the horse's belly, **not** at the sides. To ensure undue restriction on the ribcage and muscles, place the flat of your fingers between the girth and the belly as you tighten the girth.

If however, the horse is already suffering pain and soreness in the girth area, he will have attempted to tell you on numerous occasions!

The girth is not always the culprit.

- Overwork, repetition, unsuitable surfaces and continually working on one rein can lead to soreness and tightness in the girth area.

- He may show symptoms of soreness in his pectoral muscles because of pain elsewhere, such as his lower leg or foot.

The section **'Saddle fitting simplified to prevent further attack and friendly fire'**, suggested a daily gentle massage routine for your horse. If you have done a thorough job, you will now be aware of any soreness in your horse's girth area.

Below is a simple process to help you relieve your horse of soreness in the girth area:

- Stand by the horse's shoulder, preferably with a helper holding him still.

- With moderate pressure run the flat of your hand and fingers from the horse's shoulder down towards the girth area, being aware of your horse's reaction.

■ Smoothly pass your hand down the girth and around the back of his elbow. Any soreness will become immediately apparent. What appears to be a ticklish horse may in fact be soreness.

■ When placing your hand or a finger on your horse, you **must** use more pressure than a fly would when landing on him. Horses are extremely sensitive to touch. A fly will make him shudder; pain will also make him shudder.

■ Gently massage away any knots you can feel in the pectoral and surrounding muscles. He will appreciate the massage and the attention.

■ Check for any visible sores such as girth galls and act accordingly.

Reasons and signs for evasion of the saddle

I discussed this aspect in some detail throughout *'Evasion - Part 2'*. Be aware that what may appear to be evasion of the saddle, can actually start life as a problem in the mouth, and vice versa. For example:

■ The horse may hollow his back as he tries to evade an ill-fitting saddle.

■ He will also hollow his back as he lifts his head in an attempt to evade contact on the bit, which will give the appearance of an ill-fitting saddle.

■ A horse may rear for both reasons. The list goes on. Therefore, elimination of all probabilities is vital. Always look for visible clues; being hands on will give you a great deal of information such as heat, swelling, pain and so on.

The following signs of evasion are additional to those listed in *'Evasion — Part 1'*.

- An aversion to the grooming kit.

- Moving away from you as you attempt to mount up.

- Dropping his back as the saddle makes contact.

- Blowing out his belly when you attempt to fasten the girth.

- He becomes difficult for the farrier.

- As he becomes more anxious, his emotional state will begin to show.

- Overly sensitive, both physically and emotionally.

- Grumpiness.

- Stable walking.

- Re-arranging his bed.

- Wood chewing.

- Kicking at the wall.

The list goes on. There is no other reason for exposing the horse to these emotions, other than ignorance and a lack of consideration on our part.

5

The human anatomy

The significance of the human skeletal frame often
appears to be of very little relevance when in the saddle,
with emphasis placed on the muscles. The application of
both, along with simple explanations of the differences
in the male and the female skeleton, is described
in chapter 5. An interesting addition is the modest
clarification of the core muscles and other muscle groups
used when riding. *If you walk from your knees, you will
ride from your knees!* A light bulb moment for many.
The short exercises described give realisation to the
unnecessary waste of energy and effort you may exert on
your anatomy as a horse rider.

Our artillery
Your anatomy

> *"My groin really hurt the day after my lesson".*
> *"My shoulders are really stiff today after my
> lesson yesterday". "My thighs really hurt".*

Sound familiar?
The above comments are classic signs of riders abusing
their own bodies: their own **artillery** backfiring due to

a lack of preparation before the battle.

Whatever the amount of stiffness and pain you feel after riding, you will also have subjected your horse to equal measures of the same. How can you be a considerate and effective rider if your muscles are not fully charged when you begin?

Do you expect to merely jump on your horse and expect that his muscles will also be ready to work?

The human skeleton

The stability of our muscles when riding is crucial, with much emphasis given to maintaining their strength and flexibility to allow smooth and efficient movement. There appears to be very little status given to the skeleton, despite its equal significance.

The skeletal frame would be forever static if not for the pairs of muscles that provide its animation.

However, the muscles, tendons, and ligaments would be surplus to requirements if they had no skeletal frame on which to attach.

Furthermore, any mention of the human skeleton when riding often only amounts to "Sit on your seat bones"! A term often passed down with no explanation of its meaning. Novice riders will take the meaning literally; they will press their bones down into the saddle, placing pressure on two points instead of spreading the weight over the whole seat area. The discomfort can be excruciating for the horse.

- Your spine holds your head and torso upright. Although the spinal joints don't have a wide range of movement, they still allow your spine a good deal of flexibility, enabling the turn and bend of your back and neck.

- The makeup of your spine allows it to absorb shocks by the use of fibrous cartilage sandwiched between each joint in the spine that squashes under pressure, forming a cushion between the vertebrae, an excellent invention for those riders who bounce around in the saddle! Unfortunately, the horse does **not** have the luxury of the cushioning against your seat bones.

- Your spine varies in thickness and curves along its length. The protrusion points of your skull and the tailbone are directly in line with each other when your head is correctly balanced; there is no interference in the natural arch of your lower back.

- Your pelvis is a strong basin shaped ring of bones near the bottom of your spine, formed by the hipbones on the front and sides, and the triangular sacrum and coccyx on the back, which forms your tailbone. You can feel this bone at the bottom of your spine.

  - Tilt your pelvis back and forth; you will feel a certain amount of pressure. Then place it again in its natural position where there is no pressure, no tension. Be aware of any tension in this area when you are in the saddle.

- The pelvis supports your hip and thigh muscles.

- On each side of your tailbone are two protrusions; these are the seat bones.

Anatomical differences in the genders, with their various limitations and abilities, affect your lower back action and your riding.

The male rider

- You tend to have a more natural posture than the female rider.

- Your pelvis is upright and narrow, which results in a flatter back and an almost natural stable position.

■ Your almost parallel seat bones and a tailbone that tucks under the spine, make for a good deep seat that allows you to sit down with what appears to be little effort in sitting trot and canter.

■ Hip sockets which face forward, seat bones that rock freely forward and backward with the added bonus of being bow legged, allows your legs to sit naturally around the horse's barrel.

■ However, you tend to be top heavy; your centre of balance is around your waist and although this allows quite easy leg adjustments, leg stability can be hard to maintain. The top heaviness can cause you to be unbalanced.

■ Your frame tends to be heavier than the female frame. You store less fat so you usually tend to be fitter, but feel more discomfort due to your lack of padding and insulation.

■ My experience of coaching novice males has taught me that you have a tendency to use your strength when riding, which can give the impression of overpowering the horse.

■ Most males show amazement when you realise that you **don't** have to kick the horse into next week to ask him to go forward!

The female rider

■ Your pelvis on the other hand is wide; your wide seat bones and hip sockets face outwards which can force your thighs to point outwards.

■ Your tailbone is set behind the lumbar vertebrae, which causes a naturally hollow lower back. It also forces you to exert muscular energy to tuck in your tailbone, to enable you to flatten your lower back.

- The natural hollowness has a tendency to tip you forward onto your pubic bone and create an exaggerated hollow back. It not only places you in front of your centre of balance, it is also detrimental to the health of your spine.

- There is a tendency to be knock-kneed which makes it difficult for your thighs to relax, so they hang down the horse's sides rather than conforming to his barrel. This can lead to injury of tendons and ligaments.

- You have the advantage of your centre of balance being between your hipbones, making you bottom heavy, giving you a more stable lower leg.

Bony facts

Did you know that the human body has more than 300 joints? Around 230 of them are synovial joints (highly moveable joints containing a lubricant capsule such as the elbows and knees); too many joints to take care of to prevent injury!

The saddle joint in the base of your thumb allows it to move in all ways. Can you imagine how just about every aspect of the management of your horse such as holding, carrying, tying, and riding, would be affected if this joint had no movement?

If a small joint like the saddle joint could have such an effect, what influence could a malfunctioning ball and socket joint of your hip or shoulder have on your riding? Even the hinge joint of the elbow can be detrimental if the hinge has gone rusty.

Do you actively step forward from your pelvis or merely from your knees when you walk? Do you actually make full use of your skeleton?

If you walk from your knees, you will also ride from your knees!

If you don't make full use of your whole leg when walking or running, you certainly won't use it when riding. Yet you consciously strive towards the goal of your horse's engagement.

You will never reach that goal because your horse will have no choice but to mirror you.

Try the following experiment while picturing it in your mind for recall later.

- Walk as you normally would, without concentration, but being aware of the ground you cover. It feels natural and you seem to need little effort.

- Now walk again, this time imagining the ball and socket joints in your hips swinging back and forth.

- You will find that your steps cover more ground.

- You will feel that each leg swings effortlessly with very little pressure on your knees, making for long flowing strides.

- Now walk again from your knees.

- The stiffness through each leg and the pressure on your knees will be conspicuous, as will the short choppy strides you are visibly taking.

By riding from your knees, you will force your horse to take short choppy strides, placing unnecessary pressure on his knees, rather than allowing his whole leg to float with each step as you imagine the ball and socket joint in your hip swinging effortlessly with his motion.

If you have access to a bicycle, try the following:

■ As you pedal, make yourself aware of which part of your legs appears to be doing all the work. My guess is that your knees will be taking the brunt of the pressure.

■ Now, use the ball and socket of your hips to pedal. You will feel the pressure evaporate from your knees. The process will seem smoother and stress-free.

■ If you once again pedal from your knees, the difference will feel enormous.

If you think of using your frame to ride, your muscles won't have to work as hard!

Another exercise to try:

■ Lift your arm while thinking of using the muscles to set the process in motion. As I try, my arm is feeling quite heavy.

■ Now lift your arm while imagining the bones are doing the work. My arm feels much lighter and goes up with more of a spring. If you are using your imagination, yours should too.

■ Lie down on the floor and repeat the exercise with your legs. Use the same technique when in the saddle (apart from the lying down part!).

I guarantee, if you are responsible for the restriction under saddle, your horse will step up and out with you, if you simply play back the video of your experiment in your mind the next time you ride. Of course, your horse's full potential will **not** be realised if you have any more **artillery** up your sleeve! Oh, yes, here is another piece of **artillery**!

The muscles

Human muscles are comparable to the muscles of the horse. If you don't ensure the health of your horse's muscles, it is probably safe to say that you also neglect the condition of your own. Yet your muscles need to be strong to enable you to sit and to balance on your horse correctly.

The average general rider is probably not going to have correct muscle strength; this is unlikely to change if she rides only once a week, and does no other exercise. This reason, amongst many, is a cause of silent suffering in many riding school horses.

It is, however, astonishing how quickly children seem to get stronger once they take up horse riding.

Adults are a different matter. Many of us don't use our skeletal frame correctly to help us remain upright, causing us to sit heavily and slouch on the horse's back. Nor do we have the muscle strength to allow for correct movement.

The core muscles

Focus is much too often placed on the correction of the rider's seat, legs, or hands, with no mention of the core. Yet, when in the saddle, your core is as important as your heart is in keeping you alive. Your core is the structure that holds everything together. It is the backbone of an independent seat; the lower half of your body is able to absorb the horse's energy as you ask for any changes of movement, transition, or speed, and any sudden movements such as spooking.

Your core stability will allow your legs to be in contact with the horse from your seat, down through your thighs to your calf or ankle depending on the build of the horse, resulting in a stable base of support.

You use your core muscles when you sneeze and cough. Feel them as you clear your throat.

The abdominal muscles are the core of your body. When strong and aided by your skeletal frame, the core muscles will keep your physique stable and balanced. They are the mainstay regardless of your lifestyle.

■ Strong abdominal muscles will iron out any posture problems you may have.

■ Their strength will help to keep your spine correctly aligned, and protect your back.

■ Your overall health and wellbeing will improve.

■ Your confidence will improve as your body becomes straight and elegant.

■ Strong muscles improve physical performance.

■ Strong abdominals will allow your respiratory system to work more efficiently.

If your abdominal muscles are not strong and cared for:

■ Too much pressure exerted on other muscles, tendons, ligaments and joints will result in excessive wear and tear on them, and the risk of injury.

■ Your focus will fall to your shoulders as a source of balance, which will result in soreness and tiredness due to your failing efforts in balancing everything below.

■ If you don't have a good posture out of the saddle, you won't have a good posture in the saddle.

■ If you are serious about your riding and the wellbeing of both you and your horse, you should seek out a professional who can help you develop your core muscles specifically for horse riding.

- As your abdominal muscles strengthen and your spine settles into its natural shape (neutral spine), everything else becomes much easier.

Other muscle groups required in riding are those of the:

- Shoulders.

- Triceps and biceps in your upper arms.

- Back.

- Inner and outer thighs.

- Calves.

It is imperative that you don't forget the importance of your skeletal frame. If it were absent, you would simply be a messy heap on the ground!

Warming up **before** getting in the saddle is as vital as warming up in the saddle for both you and your horse in walking, and gentle muscle stretching. Cutting corners will only take you longer to achieve your goals!

6

From quicksand to solid foundations

We naturally use our voice, seat, back, legs, and hands when in the saddle. However, an awareness of efficient breathing, combined with intention, focus, feel, lightness, visualisation, and intuition plays a vital part.

Chapters 5, 6, 7, 8, and 9 are jammed packed with explanations, scenarios, remedies, and exercises that will captivate you and induce you to steer clear of the wilting weed posture, inexcusable pressures from both natural and unnatural aids, and the ugly driving seat.

The 'natural aids'!

The uses of the voice, seat, back, legs, and hands are often considered the only aids needed when in the saddle. However, an awareness of correct breathing, focus, thought, intention, and visualisation can be the most valuable of all the tools at our disposal when used positively; we are open to lightness and feel.

Your breath

Determining the primary essential of a solid foundation is quite a hard one. At first thought, it could be the mental and physical relaxation of you and the horse. The Dictionary gives the definition of **that blissful state of being at peace with oneself** (and the horse).

In the absence of relaxation, neither you nor your horse will make positive progress. Full relaxation of a useful kind will be achieved only when you are both balanced. However, until your breathing remains constant with a gentle rhythm, neither will be accomplished.

Breathing is a fundamental part of our being; we naturally breathe unconsciously. Even when we hold our breath or breathe shallowly through anxiety, nervousness, or fear, we do it unconsciously.

However, this unconscious action of holding our breath has a severe detrimental effect on the way we ride our horses, how they perform and on their wellbeing. An extremely tense horse is the product of a tense rider holding her breath. Your breath, or lack of it, is very powerful **artillery**; its negative use at any time will come back and bite you in the butt!

Nervousness encourages tension; it will stop you from breathing. Tension can occur anywhere in the body: neck, jaw, shoulders, back, elbows, wrists, fingers, hips, knees, ankles, and toes.

It is unfair to the horse:

- Tension will cause you to sit incorrectly in the saddle, displacing your weight.

- You will bounce around in the saddle as the horse goes into the faster paces.

- Initially he will try to reposition his body to accommodate yours more comfortably.

- He may become so tense that his fight or flight instinct comes into play.

- He will **not** be able to hear any commands asked of him; his focus will be on the pain you are causing him.

Think of a time when you may have got a cramp, pain, or discomfort in, for example, your leg while riding. Do you remember that you were in so much pain that you couldn't concentrate on anything else; your breathing was shallow - if you were breathing at all - and you found it difficult to communicate with your horse?

If you are stiff, in pain due to an injury, feeling nervous, or you are afraid of the horse, relaxation will be impossible. Both you and your horse will suffer the consequences.

On a particular occasion not too many years ago, I was schooling a young horse over a course of jumps. During the session, she spooked and I pulled a muscle in my leg. Initially the pain was minimal, but I ended the schooling session and decided that we should have a steady walk around the cross-country course to cool down. My horse was walking steadily along; we were having a friendly chat (as you do!). Suddenly, Ziggy stopped listening to me; she raised her head as her ears perched forward inquisitively. In turn, her back hollowed, her steps became bouncier. I then heard a low flying RAF Chinook helicopter in the distance. I tried to stay as calm and as soft as possible, whilst trying simultaneously to get her attention and to ignore the helicopter.

As Ziggy's tension and nervousness grew, I also became aware that my thigh was throbbing; the pain of my injury was becoming unbearable, I couldn't relax! Ziggy was now certainly becoming upset that not only had she a UFO to contend with; she also had a horse-eating predator on her back.

I thought it best to bail out. I sensed that Ziggy was about to literally explode; I could not so much as wrap my leg around her for security. The best thing was to let myself slide off her side as she 'went for gold'.

Suddenly - and by now the helicopter was almost overhead - it was as if someone had pulled out the plug; she completely chilled out.

Because I had decided to bail out, my mind plucked out a video I had stored some years earlier - a video I taught my pupils to use in cases of emergency. I hoped that the visualisation of my flesh now resembling melting ice cream with no skeletal frame to support it, would help me to gently slide off Ziggy's back. Suddenly every part of me became calm. I couldn't even feel the pain in my leg.

My horse literally stopped bouncing around instantly, as she too felt calm. She once again felt safe and didn't feel the need to bring her flight instinct to the fore, simply because I had restarted my natural breathing by mastering the tension in my leg, body, and mind. The Chinook carried on its journey overhead while Ziggy peacefully took us home, which leads me into your next piece of **artillery**.

Thought, imagination and visualisation

Three valuable and powerful natural aids are at your disposal any time you want them. They assist or hinder you on a daily basis, but you may not realise the power of their potential. You might say that imagination and visualisation are the same; however, visualisation gives you a clearer picture, like watching a screen. It can be stored in your mind for future reference. Practice each one regularly for dramatic improvement.

When you are thinking about tasks you must do, the images of all those tasks appear in your head; your imagination is working. If you want your horse to perform a particular movement, you will already have imagined the movement in progress.

How thought and imagination assist you:

■ **Scenario**: you are riding on a country lane and a large, very loud tractor approaches. If you calmly pass the thought to your horse *"Please walk quietly past this tractor"* or *"What a small tractor, and very quiet too"*, interpreted images will spring into your head that your horse will notice. He will walk calmly past the now very small silent tractor. However, he will be able to tell if you are not genuinely calm!

■ Think and imagine one-step ahead of where you are at that moment. Simply imagine that although the tractor is still approaching, you and your horse have already negotiated the tractor with ease.

How thought and imagination hinder you:

■ If you ride to a fence and you think, *"Please don't stop"*, your horse will likely refuse the fence due to the image you have created. This scenario would have a more positive outcome if you play a video in your head of jumping a clear round.

Using thought and imagination

Combined, thought and imagination can drastically lessen the impact of other natural **artillery** you own: voice, leg, seat, and hands.

For instance, you want your horse to go forward to a square halt from walk or trot. Simply imagine the result you want and your body will automatically begin to manoeuvre itself and assist you in asking the horse to halt. If the movement of your body doesn't bring the desired result, you may need to enhance each signal you give. Practice makes perfect!

Think of each sequence as being part of a colour palette, ranging from pure white, where the minimum pressure or contact is required, through creams and beiges, to the darker colours that require more of an ask on your part to obtain the desired effect. The more adept you are at using positive thought and imagination, the less you will need to use the darker colours.

Try this exercise:

■ Sit astride a stool; imagine sitting on the horse and ask for left lead canter. You will recognise that your right leg comes back from the hip and drops down a little more.

■ When in the saddle, try the same exercise. Be prepared for your horse to listen to your signal the moment your imagination kicks in, to prevent your body from being left behind his movement.

■ Use the same technique with various movements and paces. See yourself with the widest smile as your horse performs with perfect clarity.

Use positive thought and imagination in all areas of your riding, the handling of horses, even in your daily life; you will soon see a vast improvement generally.

Be aware that positive thinking invites positive outcomes. Negative thought will always attract negative energy. Do you have days when nothing seems to go right for you? One negative episode can set you up for attracting more of the same if you say, *"It's going to be one of those days"*! Simply acknowledge the event, let it go and imagine you are now having a wonderful day; **you *will* have a wonderful day!** Do **not** be so selfish as to allow your horse to take on board negative energy.

Being conscious of your breathing

■ If you are conscious of your breathing, you will realise that when your thought and imagery are positive, your inward breath enters from deep down in the pit of your stomach as you watch the video created by your thought. Take it a step further; imagine that your toes are nostrils; it is from here that your breath enters and leaves your body. Your horse will show his appreciation by relaxing his whole body.

- On the other hand, negative thoughts will create a horror movie combined with very little, or no breathing at all. Your horse will notice your horror movie; he will react in the instant you play it.

- With a little practice, positive thoughts and imagery will become second nature; the negative **firearm** deleted from your mind as the positive aspects play an ever-increasing part in your life as a whole!

Verbal, emotional, and physical bullying of the horse

Speak with calmness and understanding, your horse will literally understand and believe every word you say. He will relish your kindness; he will trust you. Raise your voice and negative energy will pass between you.

Your voice has the potential to be a malicious piece of **artillery** in its tone and the by words you speak. Please believe me when I say that your horse will understand and believe any arrogant and derogatory remark that passes your lips in his direction!

Horses suffer the same emotional stress that we do. As a child, were you bullied? Were you ever the victim of a malicious remark that still has an emotional hold over you? Maybe your emotional problems caused you to be irrational.

Behavioural problems quite often manifest in children when they are, for example, unable to cope with emotional trauma. Horses exhibit behavioural problems when they are no longer able to cope with the emotional and physical trauma we place on them.

While you may be referred to a professional specialising in psychological issues, you may send your horse off to a trainer! He may have responded positively to all manner of training methods and returned a very well behaved horse.

However, the core issue, the true problem will still be there. It may lay dormant for a while, but just one memory of his traumatic past will be enough to shoot it from its hibernation. Your horse will go back to square one the moment you repeat the event. Will you then surrender him to yet more emotional strain when you hang a 'for sale' sign around his neck with the label **'unpredictable'** attached?

Equine Holistic practitioners have the ability to help the horse rid himself of his emotional baggage; in turn the often-related physical manifestation, such as lameness and skin conditions miraculously often disappears!

Your horse may be harbouring years of emotional rubbish due to any of the following examples as well as many others not listed.

- The use of **artillery**.

- Injuries and physical trauma that have gone unnoticed.

- Being suddenly whisked from his mother.

- The loss of his best friend.

- Being housed next door to a bully.

- Moving from home to home.

- A traumatic experience while travelling.

Clear communication – or the lack of it

Clear communication is the pinnacle of our aims. During an exam some years ago, I, and my co-candidates were asked, *"Which comes first – balance, rhythm, impulsion or tempo?"* Everyone in turn, gave their answer, confident in their manner.

I immediately but sheepishly remarked, *"None of those, it has to be communication"*. For a moment, I wanted the ground to swallow me up as the examiner glared at me while the group looked on in awe that I had dared to rock the boat.

"Explain", was the sarcastic tone. Below was my reply.

> *"Well, none of them are possible without clear communication between both the horse and rider. If the rider isn't clear in asking her horse to get a move on, he won't engage his hindquarters in preparation for what comes next. Maybe he is unable to respond due to restriction, pain, or discomfort. How does he communicate this - without risking punishment - to a rider who has a whip at the ready because she was taught that her legs, hands, body, seat, voice, whips and spurs, are the only communication required? The only response required from the horse is just that — a response; the whip is ready and waiting should he give a wrong answer"!*

Blimey! I could see by the bewilderment on their faces that the group were unfamiliar with any kind of detriment the horse could possibly suffer. My outburst was awarded with the contempt it did **not** deserve!

If your horse continues to show his distaste at you sitting on his back, in spite of all the positive outcomes of checking his health, the saddle, bridle and so on, the problem likely lies with your posture, or your riding ability may not be a suitable match for the horse.

Your posture – wilting weed

You may hear echoes of the importance of your posture and the correct ear, shoulder, hip and heel line, as well as the alignment of the centre of the back of your head, spine, cantle, the horse's spine, and tail.

First time encounters with experienced pupils continue to clarify in me their lack of understanding of the significance of a correct posture and a strong core when riding horses, as opposed to the human posture and core generally. I gave basic guidance on the core muscles earlier. Below is a simple account of the horse rider's posture.

- Your body naturally works in such a way as to allow you to maintain balance as you stand, sit, walk, kneel, lie down, cross your legs, lean every which way, even to stand on your head if you want to. You have nurtured and built up your own muscle strength to achieve your body's various repetitious positions and movements. Even if only resting in an armchair, your core muscles automatically help to keep your body stable.

- Once you are in the desired position and become still, the muscles can rest.

- Horse riding is not a pastime that allows you to remain completely still. Even though we endeavour to appear to be sitting still and soft in the saddle, while using as little effort as possible to achieve our desires, our core muscles are in fact constantly on the go, trying to keep our bodies from sliding off the saddle. They are forced to work harder if the horse is bouncy, or he spooks, pulls and so on. The effort spent on building our muscles to enable us to do all the day-to-day stuff out of the saddle, is far from adequate for our stability and core strength when in the saddle. Ideally, specific training will build up the muscles that lie deep within your core. However, I realise that you may lack the time or the means, particularly if you are not a serious competitor; in which case I have listed further on some simple common exercises to help improve specific areas of your body.

- The large gym balls are an excellent aid to the correct build of muscle; however, an expert trainer should guide you.

- The symmetry of your hips and being strong through your core muscles is essential to good posture and in turn, a balanced seat. Lop-sidedness can be cured; however, you will feel very uncomfortable for a little while as your body goes through the process of being moulded into positions that are alien to it. Perseverance and an expert who understands the biomechanics of riding will assist you in your enormous positive transformation.

- Any hint of rider unbalance, whether it is due to your asymmetry or unfitness, affects your whole body and radically reduces effective communication between you and your horse. Imagine a person is speaking to you on the phone, but due to interference on the line her words are intermittent, very frustrating; I rest my case!

- The more unbalanced you are, the more you will move around in the saddle, placing ever more trauma on the horse's back, muscles and joints, as he constantly tries to re-balance himself.

While you are snuggling into your armchair taking in all this fascinating information, try the following exercise:

- Imagine you are sitting on your horse.

- Lift your knees so that you are sitting on your seat bones only. Unless you are strong through your core and normally quite balanced sitting on a horse, the odds are that your arms are up in the air as you try to balance your body, or, you are gripping the arms of the chair, your lower back is stiff, and you are leaning back onto the back of the chair for support.

- Whether your hands are in the air or grabbing the chair arms, if you were on a horse, it would be his mouth and back that would now be suffering.

- Let your legs touch down again and sit as you were.

- Be aware of your now broad and stable base of support as you sit not only on your seat bones, but also through the back of your thighs. There is no gap from your seat down the length of the back of your thighs as you sit in your chair.

The principle is the same when you are sitting on the horse; the only difference is that your inner thigh will be in contact as opposed to the back of the thigh.

The independent seat and the ugly driving seat

It follows, that through the strengthening of your core muscles your pelvis is supported in the correct position without the hindrance and abuse of the reins, enabling a flowing connection with the horse's movement, balance, coordination, and energy.

Your stable core allows everything around it to move independently without any loss of balance. You feel secure in the knowledge that wherever your horse goes, you will remain connected and flowing through your hips. The use of your seat is almost invisible as your horse appears to dance effortlessly forward.

Your legs are free to employ as required without tension. Your rein contact gives you the confidence of remaining in balance if you were to let go of the reins.

Yet have you noticed that some dressage riders tilt their pelvis forward so that their seat bones dig deep into the saddle; they are sitting on the back of their buttocks and their tailbone. The whole of the rider's lower back is slumped, but the horse is really stretching out with his front legs? Do you consider this pose to be a work of art in the dressage arena?

If force is used, the horse will feel discomfort or even worse, pain. He may appear to go forward energetically; sadly, he is making vain attempts at moving away from the pain that is constant and remains so for as long as the rider desires.

You may have noticed show jumpers and event riders using the same driving seat on the approach to a fence if the horse starts to back off.

The use of the aggressive driving seat is still common practice amongst some of the top riders, though thankfully it appears to be declining as the younger generations come through the ranks. It can be so attacking to the horse that he puts quite a spurt on, only to meet with an aggressive blocking rein.

You may have often seen a horse that is backing away from something of which he is unsure. The rider may be using the same driving seat. The horse will try to be brave as he darts past the obstacle under duress; the next time, he will remember the pain caused by that obstacle!

Many mentors and writers of books will advise you to take notice of how a top rider may sit on and ride her horse, to aspire to that rider and imagine that you are riding your horse in the same way. It is excellent advice, as long as the rider you aspire to sits correctly and asks rather than forces the horse.

You may have been told that there is no point in wishing and visualising you ride like Charlotte Dujardin if your physique pays no resemblance to hers. I beg to differ on that opinion. A positive attitude, positive energy, and good visualisation won't magically alter your physique; they will however, boost your confidence and enhance your emotional and physical wellbeing, causing an all-round better performance.

If you are unable to maintain an independent seat:

- Your body will stiffen; your hips, thighs, and lower legs will react like a vice.

- Your various body parts will not be able to work independently of each other.

- Due to the incorrect hip and ankle alignment, your legs will not remain steady under your torso. Rising trot will be very difficult for you. You may therefore try to sit to the trot, which will be most uncomfortable for both of you, and detrimental to the health of the horse's back.

- You may tip forward onto your fork; your unbalanced weight will force the horse onto his forehand causing him to lose balance. He needs to maintain his balance over his centre so that he can carry the heavy weight of his head and neck. However, he will now have your added weight too!

- You may fall backward, placing your body behind the horse's movement, causing him to lose his balance in his quarters. Your legs will tip forward, forming a chair seat. Inevitably, your reins will follow your hands as your body falls back, only to be stopped in their tracks by the bit bulldozing the contents of the horse's mouth.

- Your breathing may become shallow, even stop, causing more tension.

- Existing tension may begin to manifest as pain.

- As your tension grows, your legs will lift, causing your feet to slide precariously around on your stirrups. You may even lose your stirrups completely.

- You will probably fall off. Your stiffness may cause injury as you land.

- Your confidence may be shattered.

How will the horse react?

■ The horse will mirror your stiffness. He will feel blocked throughout his body.

■ He will show the typical signs of discomfort.

■ If his behaviours don't alert you to his misery, the horse will become agitated; he will develop wrongly diagnosed **behavioural issues**, or his performance will become dull and lifeless as he switches off.

■ He will have the label of being **hard in the mouth**, **stubborn**, or **dead to your leg**.

■ At the very least, he will suffer soreness from the tip of his mouth, through his whole body and legs.

■ Have you noticed at any time when riding, that the horse may run forward or he may stop? Do you know why? Do you think he is being naughty or stubborn? **Actually, he is merely trying to reposition you over his centre where it feels comfortable for him to carry your weight.**

Anything the horse does is usually
down to you, the rider!

7

Exercises to promote an independent seat

I t is crucial that the horse is not the subject of indiscriminate distress during your exercise regime. I have seen far too many school horses suffer at the hands of beginner and novice riders bouncing around in the saddle, while simultaneously juggling with the reins as they make futile attempts at directing the horse and his motion.

These riders are **NOT** taught how to ride; they are merely shown **abusive skills** in how to make their horses move from the **kick** of the leg and to stop at the **pull** of the rein!

If you are in this category, I urge you to insist on having a leader so that you have the freedom to concentrate solely on learning the art of riding through **balance and harmony**.

Do not attempt exercises that require you to let go of the reins unless you are in an enclosed area and have someone to assist you.

If holding onto the pommel, place three or four fingers of each hand on the underside, **leaving the palms of your hands free,** so as to prevent the creation of an angle at your wrists. The angle would result in tension and stiffness through the length of your arms; it may also cause you to tip forward, putting weight on the horse's forehand, making it difficult for him to move forward freely.

During the exercises, remain elegant and remember that the source of balance is from your core, not from your shoulders!

Standing on the stirrups – promotes good balance

The exercise will test your breathing technique, relaxation, balance, an awareness of the natural placement of your centre of gravity and of your lower leg. Perform the exercise during your warm up in the saddle and throughout the session. Mastery of the exercise is necessary at halt prior to its use through the paces.

Any exercise involving standing on the stirrups gives you a head start in improving your balance for all round performance. The lower your centre of gravity is, the sturdier your base of support will be. Refrain from any rein contact when carrying out the exercise until you are able to balance independently. It is appropriate to hold onto lots of mane to begin with.

- Don't complicate things by trying to use the whole of your body to stand. Use your imagination. How do you rise from a chair or a stool? It is as simple as that. Ensure your head and neck balance correctly on your shoulders.

- Ensure that your stirrups are not so long that your crotch collides with the pommel as you rise up. Unbalance and weak lower legs will result from stirrups that are too long.

  1. Rise up from the saddle, simultaneously gently sinking down into your heels without moving your lower legs away from the horse.

      Do **not** force the heels down to the point that you feel pressure in your ankles. Repeat frequently.

2. Try pinching with your knees, thighs or the back of your calves to experience how **bracing** can raise your centre of gravity and change the location of your body weight.

   Be aware of your horse's reaction. He will mirror your every move.

3. Vary the standing positions from folding at the hips, to standing straight up. Keep the angles clean, your back straight with your neck and head flowing out from your shoulders.

4. Test your balance further by bending your knees, gradually closing and opening the angle at the back of your knees to varying degrees.

5. Crouch down so that your bottom is almost touching the saddle.

6. Remember to slide your bottom towards the cantle so that your torso is able to balance easily over your thighs. Your head and neck again flowing out from your shoulders that should lie gently back.

7. Work on moving your torso around as you keep your legs still, soft, and equally balanced underneath you.

8. Place your arms in various positions: on your head, hips, folding in front of your body, behind your body and so on.

9. There are lots of balancing exercises you can do out of the saddle. Seek them out if you have none of your own.

Result: suppleness in your ankles is developed. You will begin to feel more secure in the saddle as your centre of gravity settles into its home. The exercise helps to unlock your lower back.

You may struggle with the exercises if:

- You try to use your whole body to stand up.

- You stop breathing.

- You grip with your legs.

- You stiffen through your back.

- You try to straighten your knees as you stand up.

- You tip your toes and head.

- You try to use the horse's mane or neck strap to pull yourself up.

How to obtain a deeper seat, lower your centre of gravity, and remain in balance

1. Take your thighs slightly away from the saddle as if doing the splits; you must be careful not to overdo it as you may get cramp. Your seat remains relaxed.

   As your thighs again make contact with the saddle, gently slide them forward so that your thigh muscles press to the back of your legs, allowing them to lie flat against the saddle.

   It is also a worthy exercise if you grip with your knees and thighs, and bring your legs too far forward.

2. Focusing on one leg at a time, conjure up a picture of a dog cocking a back leg at its favourite tree and mimic the image.

3. Perform the motion of pedalling a bicycle forwards then backwards. Do **not** lean back when pedalling.

4. Holding on to the pommel, slide your knees up to the pommel, like a jockey.

5. Test your balance and posture by letting go of the pommel while bringing your knees closer together. Gently drop your knees back down under your body.

The exercise also allows your bottom to drop deeper into the saddle.

6. A horse not going forward correctly or not going in a straight line is usually the result of tension in the rider. As you ride your horse, tense the various muscles. Take note of how you feel and watch for any reaction in your horse.

How to improve lower body and limb problems

How to correct hip problems

Any hip problems such as sitting crookedly stem from the pelvis. One hip collapses giving the impression of uneven stirrups.

1. First, you must find your seat bones and buttocks to enable you to distribute your weight evenly; sit on your hands and wriggle about in the saddle to help you feel your seat bones.

Think of spreading your weight, along with your buttocks, evenly across the saddle and not simply thinking of your seat bones pointing downwards.

2. If you have a tendency to collapse to the right, look over your right shoulder (without twisting your hips), to the horse's tail and then look ahead again. Your hips immediately become square on.

If collapsing to the left, look over your left shoulder.

3. Bring your knees up after taking your feet out of the stirrups. You will feel you are sitting deeper in the

saddle. As you bring your knees back down, pull the fat of your inner thigh from behind so that it rests as flat as possible against the saddle.

Result: your body will be straight and flawless.

How to stretch your back and legs

1. Without stirrups and with the reins in one hand, slowly stretch your free arm up as high as possible while stretching your legs down and pointing your toes to the ground. Your toes come back up, levelling the heel and producing freedom from tension. Repeat the exercise swapping the reins over to your other hand. Keep your torso straight.

2. Imagine you are riding a bicycle. Cycle quite fast while stretching, and lengthening your entire leg.

3. Take away your legs from the horse's sides, and then gently place them back on.

Result: your legs are secure around the horse's barrel. Balance is maintained, and the horse's rhythm will feel more even.

How to stretch your thigh muscles

1. Facing forward, lift up behind you each lower leg in turn, cup it in your hand just above your ankle, then pull your lower leg up towards your bottom. You should feel the muscle in the front of your thigh stretching, but it must be as soft as possible.

    Visualise the ball and socket at the top of the femur (thighbone) rotating to allow your leg to come back.

How to correct lower leg problems

Problems arise in the lower legs when you are unable to secure them around the horse's sides. Your lower legs tend to swing loosely backward and forward in a seesaw effect instead of being still, resulting in tension in your lower back and the motion of the horse being impeded.

How to keep your knees in the correct position

1. Bring both feet up behind the saddle; the movement will pull your knees back into the correct position.

2. Then let your feet gently and naturally drop; your knees must remain in the position already achieved, with your toes just behind them.

    If you struggle to keep your knees still during the exercise, ask your helper to lay the palm of her hand in front of one knee to prevent it from coming forward as you drop your foot. With repetition, you will soon get the hang of it.

    Your body must remain upright and, providing you are sitting softly with no tension in your back, a good natural curve in your back is assured.

3. Touch the toes of your right foot with your right hand, then your left toes with your left hand. Your lower leg must be still and underneath your body.

4. With knees and lower legs still, bring your right hand over to touch the toes of your left foot and vice versa. Point your nose to your knee while maintaining equal weight across your hips.

    Don't lean to the side of the horse or step onto the stirrup on that side. Both will pull the horse out of balance. You may also lose your balance and fall off the saddle. Therefore, as you move your body over to touch your toes on a particular foot, use imagery to help your hips remain stable, such as impeccably balanced weigh scales. It will become easier with practice and as your suppleness improves. Asking your helper to place the palm of her hand in front of your toes will assist in keeping your toes and lower leg in place.

The leg moving back is a common fault during this exercise, which will cause you to tip forward and lose your balance. Ask your helper to hold your foot in place if this fault should occur.

5. Test your ability to maintain your leg position by placing your hands on your hips as you lean forward as far as possible from your hips, keeping the lower half of your body still.

6. Lying back on the horse - if he is agreeable and with assistance - will test the security of your lower leg. As you lie back, your lower leg should be still and underneath your body.

Often, the legs have a tendency to move forward and the heels may come up slightly due to tension in the lower back, which may also cause its natural arch to deepen. Ask your helper to reposition your legs if this problem should occur. You will soon develop the correct feel.

The angle of your leg and foot – east v west!

How often have you been told to point your toes forward, to find that they drift back to their east and west position?

It is a fact that many riders have feet that point outwards and nothing short of amputation and repositioning will ever get them to point their toes to the front. If you try to point your toes forward but your feet naturally splay outwards, the following will result:

- You will have to bend your ankles to achieve the desired effect.

- This action will cause your feet to bend inwards with the soles on an incline facing each other.

- The weight will be forced onto the outside of your foot, and the little toe and its ball, instead of the ball of the big toe.

- The muscles in your lower leg will also tense up. The horse will mirror the effect.

Unless you compete seriously, it isn't essential that your toes point to the front.

Importance in this instance lies with the position of your legs. A plumb line that aligns with your shinbone through its length from your knee to your foot will confirm the correct placement of your leg. You may find that on a wide horse, your pelvis may force your legs out from the knee.

If you are not a victim of splayed feet but you tend to point your toes outwards, the following will occur:

- Your legs will also point outwards resulting in a gap between your legs and the horse.

- Rather than your calf resting on the horse, your ankle and heel will be in contact with the horse's belly, resulting in more aggressive leg pressure than intended because the pressure will focus on a smaller bearing surface than if coming from the calf.

- You will attempt to stabilise yourself by sitting solely on your seat bones with no support from your legs, making your seat very unstable.

■ The tiny base of support that your seat bones allow will bear down onto the horse's back, causing discomfort.

Try the following exercise:

■ With your legs away from the saddle, alternately swing your lower legs from your knees backwards and forwards. Your knees should remain in their usual position.

How to improve upper body and limb problems

Several upper body problems come from tension or bad posture. Tension in your head and neck is a major problem as your head strains forward and unbalances your entire body.

Rounded shoulders lead to a slouched back. The movement of the horse is then forced through your upper body instead of through the small of your back. If you are not loose in your waist, your feet will **not** be still.

How to ease tension in your head, face, and neck

1. Turn your head slowly from side to side, keeping your body facing ahead.

2. Gently and slowly bring your head down; touch your chin to your chest, allowing your head to drop and hang like a dead weight to help stretch your spine.

3. Then bring your head back as far as it will go without force, but letting it hang off the back of your neck to open the front of your body.

4. Next, bring your head forward to the upright position. Gently and slowly, aim to touch your left shoulder with your left ear, and then gently sweep

your head over to repeat the exercise with your right shoulder and ear. **Don't** raise your shoulder to meet your ear! **Don't** put any force into the exercise if you are unable to make contact to begin with. Suppleness will result if done regularly.

5. Draw the largest figure of eight possible with your nose while facing ahead, to relax your neck muscles.

    Perform slowly to avoid injury and dizziness.

6. Roll your head in a circle from one shoulder to the other. It must be carried out slowly so as not to cause any dizziness.

How to straighten and ease tension in your shoulders, waist and improve posture

1. Shrug your shoulders up to your ears, then rotate them back and down. Think of circling your shoulders like a wheel going backwards.

2. Ride with your hands on your head; then touch your shoulders. Your elbows should remain far enough back so that you can't see them.

3. Fold your arms behind your back as high up as is comfortable.

4. Elevate your rib cage and stretch your abdomen by pushing your shoulder blades closer together, flattening them into your back. You will feel that your torso is lifting.

Result: your upper arms hang softly while your elbows remain low and steady.

1. Stretch both arms out sideways to shoulder height; you will feel your diaphragm lift; stretch them out in front of you, then stretch upwards with one arm at a time as if climbing a ladder.

2. With the reins in one hand, let your opposite arm hang by your side. Then, with your buttocks remaining securely and equally weighted in the saddle, swing your arm forwards, backwards, forwards then up and over in a constant rhythm.

   Change over to your other arm.

3. Stretch out your arms at shoulder height imitating an aeroplane; swing your upper body and head slowly from side to side.

   Don't move your bottom or collapse through your waist. Your legs should be still and underneath your body.

4. Sitting up straight with your hands on your waist, your head up and facing ahead, swing your right elbow and shoulder forward while allowing the left elbow and shoulder to go back.

5. Gently and slowly stretch, just like when you get out of bed.

6. Punch the air softly in all directions especially upwards and backwards, to loosen your shoulder and back muscles.

Result: your shoulders are no longer slouched; your head, neck, and waist are relaxed.

The following exercise encourages a naturally arched lower back; it also correctly aligns the inside shoulder:

1. Take the reins into your outside hand. Fold your inside hand behind your back, cupping your hand around the bend of the elbow of your outside arm.

    Gently push your folded arm into your lower back.

How to correct hand problems

Tension and rigidity of the arms is a major problem that causes the reins to flap, resulting in the horse being visibly uncomfortable around his mouth.

You may subconsciously support your arm from the shoulder rather than let it hang, which will cause tension from your shoulder through to the horse's mouth as well as down through your torso.

A tell-tale sign of supporting your arm through your shoulder is the rising of your elbow as your seat leaves the saddle in the rising trot, or a jerking of the rein on the bit due to your lack of an elastic rein contact.

Ride in a constant energetic rhythm, letting your arms flow with the rhythm as each of the horse's legs steps forward.

1. Hold your reins in one hand and raise the other arm to shoulder level. Practice the exercise first in walk, then in trot.

2. Place a whip between each thumb and index finger; bend your elbows as you ride to the walk then to the trot while keeping the whip level. This is an exceptional exercise for steadying the hands.

    It is also the most practical use of the **whip**!

3. In each hand, hold a plastic cup containing water, while keeping an elastic, sensitive, and allowing

contact on the reins as your horse walks on. The cup must remain steady so that no water escapes.

The reins will straighten as you begin to carry your hands more effectively.

4. Loosen your wrists and fingers by shaking your hands when they are free of the reins.

Result: you will sit correctly with your weight evenly distributed, and your spine aligned with your centre of gravity.

Newsflash!

A major problem that appears to go unnoticed is the forward motion of the rider's elbows as they follow her body when rising to the trot, yet the horse's head is quite static in this gait. The following will occur if you are guilty of this fault:

- Contact is lost through the rein as your elbows follow your torso when you rise out of your saddle in the standing phase of the trot.

- On the downward sequence, the reins may pull on the bit as your seat connects with the saddle.

Solution: As your seat leaves the saddle, leave your elbows in their natural resting position: each shoulder to elbow remains vertically placed, your elbow to your hand remains an extension of the rein.

Effectively, as you rise, your torso will move forward of your elbows. There will be no adverse movement or jerking of the reins.

How to test general balance

A sequence of standing on the stirrups, combined with aspects of the previous exercises will test your balance and self-control.

How to correct the chair seat

The chair seat is one of the most common problems: your feet are too far forward rather than directly underneath your hips. It creates problems because you can easily get behind the movement of the horse, causing your body to tip backwards and your legs to grip upwards.

You may have been informed that it is because the lower leg has come forward. However, the cause is often due to the rider sitting too far back in the saddle. In this position, you will have too much weight on your seat bones. There is no straight line from your hip to your heel.

Having determined that the saddle fits correctly, the following exercises are helpful.

1. Stand up in your stirrups so that your seat is above the pommel with your hips well forward. You must balance without hindering the horse through the reins and without gripping with your knees.

    If you are successful in this quest, your legs will be directly underneath your body.

    Slide down the pommel, sitting very slowly and gently back in the saddle seat, with your feet remaining in the position achieved.

    Repeat the above exercise regularly, because your seat for a while will have a tendency to move back to what it considers a comfortable position. Your lower legs will become stiff and tense as they force their weight down into your feet again!

2. Take away your stirrups and cross them over the saddle in front of you. Wriggle around in the saddle to feel your seat bones and your buttocks. Imagine where the back pockets would be if you were

wearing a pair of jeans. The bottom of the pockets would be touching the saddle.

You may have been advised that you must feel your three points: the two seat bones and the pubic bone. I will discuss this in the next problem.

3. Circle your ankles towards the horse to relax your hips.

4. Swing your lower legs to relax and open your hips: as one leg goes back, the other swings forward as you keep your toes in and your heels out to prevent you from inadvertently kicking the horse.

5. To strengthen and open your hips and pelvis, hold on to the front of the saddle with one hand; with the other hand grab your ankle and point your knee to the ground, only as far as is comfortable.

    Hold the position, relax, and repeat with the other leg.

6. To stretch your hips and flexor muscles, hold both reins in one hand; raise both legs to the top of the saddle, then push both legs back and down towards the horse's hocks without tipping forward.

Result: your legs align from the hip to the heel.

How to correct the fork seat

The opposite of the chair seat; Instead of sitting on the seat bones and buttocks, you tend to sit more on the pubic bone, bringing a little weight back to the seat bones; this causes your lower back to hollow and inhibits the combined mobility of you and the horse.

1. Simply **'sit on your pockets'** while maintaining the openness through your chest and lightness through

your waist, as well as relaxing your lower back. Not only will you be a more relaxed rider, the horse will be relieved.

Revert to your normal position and note the difference.

When sitting on your fork, your pelvis tips back, which puts the pressure of the two seat bones on the horse's back. It also forces your lower back into an unnatural curve.

When sitting on your pockets, your pelvis tips forward, giving a much softer and secure feeling all around. **Don't** force your pelvis forward.

Exercises from the ground

Test your balance:

1.   Stand on one leg; hop on one leg. Repeat with both legs.

2.   Squat on the floor and remain in balance. Try this exercise against a wall to begin with to help keep your body straight and build your strength.

     If you struggle to balance during the exercise, you will also struggle to maintain your balance when in the saddle.

3.   You will get the feel of how your position should be in the saddle by standing with your back straight against a level wall, with your shoulders, bottom, and heels touching the wall. Your head should be raised and level.

     Stand on a book, only as thick and sufficient distance from the wall to allow you drop your heel slightly. Bend your knees slightly.

The more frequently you perform this exercise, the quicker you will learn to feel the correct position in the saddle.

4. Take notice of the way you walk. Make a note of your posture in a mirror. Are you round shouldered? Do you slump from your hips when sitting in a chair or on the floor? If you do, you will also do it when sitting on a horse.

5. Imagine you are sitting straight up with a relaxed back, shoulders are square and relaxed; allow your hips to move loosely.

6. Walk around with a book resting on your head.

7. When you are able to balance a book on your head and to create an elegant posture, try walking forward while slumping from the shoulders and hips. Can you feel the tension through your lower back and leg muscles?

8. Lean back and walk. Can you feel those tendons stretching in your legs and the discomfort as the arch in your lower back is exaggerated?

9. Stand at the edge of a very low step, first aiming to balance on the balls of your feet and your toes.

    Bring the weight back to your heels; you will feel the tension in your calf muscles dissipate; you will feel more secure through your balance.

8

Inexcusable pressures

Have you ever actually thought about the term 'aid'? The term is a synonym for 'help, assist, support, relief, encourage, benefit'. Consider for a moment what its meaning conjures up for you as an individual.

For me, the term has never sat well, although I did conform to a certain degree as I came up through the ranks of coaching.

If we 'aid' our horses, how can we have the audacity to turn the aid into a pressure, such as the pressure from our legs and hands, or pressure from a weight such as the weight of our body on his back, or a burden that can range from an unbalanced rider to the general stress we place on him?

We don't aid the horse through his movements; we control him! I am no less guilty than any other rider is. Nonetheless, I strive to make my connections with the horses I ride as simple as possible. My following adage sums it up.

Horses are not robots, but we try to program them by constantly using the same aids regardless.

Your weight imbalance

It is important to understand that a constant pressure goes away, for example, the girth's pressure on the horse's belly. Initially, a young horse may be apprehensive about the pressure of the girth, but because the pressure never changes, he starts to ignore it.

If you inadvertently apply constant pressure with your leg, seat, weight or hand, the horse soon learns to ignore the pressure. That is why development of an independent seat through relaxation, muscle and skeletal strength, balance and an ability to stay with the horse's motion is crucial to proper application of the connections.

As a horse will begin to ignore constant pressure from your seat, leg and hand, he will also begin to ignore your constant uneven weight distribution, resulting in him becoming less sensitive.

Are you unbalanced?

SCENARIO:

■ On feeling your connection, the horse willingly responds to the pressure. On completion of the movement, the pressure doesn't change so he again responds, each time trying to re-balance himself under your body.

■ As the pressure remains constant, even though he has done his job, he becomes confused as his questions go unheeded. The horse gives subtle hints in an attempt to get your attention. Sadly, you continue to ignore him.

Constant subjection to your imbalance will give him no choice but to try to ignore the discomfort; he will go through life trying to make the best of a bad situation.

His uncomfortable forced position will eventually no longer be alien to him; he will become accustomed to it, just as he is accustomed to the constant pressure of his girth.

- You will have difficulty keeping the horse straight as your uneven weight continues to force him to stride along, while his body bends away from the pressure.

- In turn, you will keep a constant pressure on the opposite rein in a vain attempt to keep him on track, oblivious to the damage occurring underneath you because the horse will still canter, gallop, and jump for you. However, he will not perform to his full potential due to his forced crookedness; punishment may follow.

Your bad posture will only come to light when you are capable of recognising it, or if you ride a well-schooled horse that is sensitive to your 'aids'. Watch your step because you will **not** be tolerated!

Pressure from your legs

Invariably, the horse and rider get frustrated with each other, often because we try too hard with our connections. We are brainwashed into believing that a set 'aid' must be given in order for the horse to perform a particular exercise; we must use our legs in all sorts of ways and in specific positions with varying amounts of pressure from passive to disrespectfully kicking the horse. If the outcome is dire, we just have to do the same painstaking drill repeatedly until it improves.

Your riding will eventually 'appear' to improve, but only when the horse has become so tired of trying to teach you the correct way, that he gives up and complies with anything on offer, even the **kick, kick, kick** of your legs.

If we were able to unscrew our legs above the knee, our riding would much improve; our horses would have the freedom to feel, to understand, and to carry out the job asked of them!

"You must put your outside leg back behind the girth when bending the horse". If you fail to do so, the world might end!

Further in the guide, I will take you through a process so simple, yet so effective, you will advance in no time at all!

Pressure from your hands

The subtle use of the reins is a vital component in the art of classical dressage, but far too frequently used by general riders who give them precedence over the seat connections.

The reins regularly and incorrectly steer the horse.

Despite the still often erroneously used phrase *"Pull your inside rein back towards your knee"* when turning the horse, the correct term is *"Open the inside rein and invite the horse into the space"*! Using the inside rein is simply a means of asking and helping the horse to travel in the direction requested by you.

We are taught that the reins control the horse's head. I put the following to you:

when we are sufficiently balanced, we allow the horse the freedom to maintain his balance. He will control his own head.

The manipulation of the horse's head with your hands and reins will throw him off balance. When in the saddle, your hands should be at the back of the queue in the line of **artillery**. However, if you fail to encourage the horse in using his energy to transport himself forward from his hindquarters due to your own inaccuracy, you will be forever closing the front door on him as you constantly pull on the reins due to your destabilised body.

By pulling on the inside rein:

■ You inhibit the engagement of the horse's inside hind leg as you disconnect him.

■ The horse may turn his nose, but his outside shoulder will continue straight on.

■ The pull on his mouth will cause him to take evasive action.

■ The shifting backwards of the inside seat bone often accompanies a pulling back of the rein on the same side, contradicting the aid wanted.

■ The shifting of the weight can also cause your leg to go forward, resulting in your loss of balance.

In reality, the inside rein moves only as far away from the horse's neck as the outside rein can move towards the neck without being brought over the mane. However, a more open rein can often assist a green horse and a novice rider in their learning process.

■ Your shoulders come around no further than your hips. Your hands and arms come around together with no more force on one rein than the other.

■ Think of when riding a bicycle: if you want to turn left, you bring the handlebars round to the left; as the left bar comes around towards your body, the right bar moves away from your body in equal measure.

■ If you tried to pull the left handle bar too quickly without support from the right bar, the wheel would come too far round, throwing you off course, unbalancing you with possible disastrous results.

■ However, if you tried to hold the right handle bar still while you attempted to bring the left bar towards you, your bicycle would **not** turn. If you had too much pressure on the right handle bar, your bicycle would probably start to wobble.

The only redeeming quality here is that the bicycle being an inanimate object would not become confused or distressed!

A major problem that often goes unseen is that of riders holding their reins as if holding bicycle handlebars. **Try the following exercise:**

- Hold your reins correctly: as if holding the handle of a mug, with your fingers gently wrapped around the reins, fingertips gently touching the palms of your hands and the reins secured between the underside of your thumbs and the middle joints of your index fingers.

- With your thumbs uppermost, feel the joints of your wrists relax as your hands drop into a natural relaxed position.

- Now turn your hands so that your thumbnails face each other. Can you feel the tension along the outside length of your forearms?

  The horse will feel in his mouth the same tension you experience.

If we were able to unscrew our arms from the shoulders, our riding would much improve!

Are you aware that if you could unscrew your arms and throw them away, you would still have the ability to slow and stop your horse, if he has no reason to distrust you?

9

Inexcusable artificial artillery

The possibility of failure in dominating the horse is not an option for the human species. If he will not succumb to the power of our anatomy, we attach spurs to our boots and fill our hands with whips.

Spurs

The 'verb' (meaning an action) in the Oxford Dictionary for spur is **urge** (a horse) **forward by digging one's spurs into its sides.**

Spurs are another creation in the name of human dominance over the horse as our ancestors jabbed him in the stomach as a reminder that he must obey and move if he was to avoid any pain.

Spurs are mandatory at the highest levels of British dressage. The rules forbid their 'excessive' use. The rules also allow the wearing of spurs at all lower levels of dressage.

The justification for the use of spurs in any discipline and at any level is highly contentious.

The horse's skin resembles that of a rhino!

The above belief is merely a 'get out of jail' card for avoiding the truth that his skin is actually extremely sensitive.

A pilot study by Dr Lydia Tong MA VetMB Veterinary Pathologist confirms that the underlying layer of the horse's skin (dermis) is less than 1mm thicker than that of human skin. Crucially, the top layer (epidermis) that houses the pain-sensing nerve fibres is thinner than human skin.

If you wear spurs, would you contemplate targeting your ribs with a spur? Now being made aware that your own skin is less sensitive than that of your horse will you continue to spur him?

However, whereas you may have uttered an expletive, the horse - being a prey animal - would appear weak in front of you, the predator, if he was to utter any sound of pain. His survival instinct forces the impression of a strong horse; he will continue to face his abuse in silence.

His silence is often his ruin, because we don't pause to consider the exploitation we impose on him. Yet, if he were to object, he would be punished.

Signs of spur abuse:

■ Hair loss and changes of skin colour just behind the girth or under the belly, depending on the length of the rider's legs.

■ Gashes.

■ Bumps that resemble 'hives' or bites. It can be difficult to confirm that bumps are because of spur abuse and not merely bites. However, your recognition of the regular positioning of your spurs and your conscience will be your judge.

The horse's mental state can be greatly affected by spur abuse; it is vital that he is permitted to go back to the point he feels sufficiently at ease to release his emotional garbage, and then restart the learning process at his pace. He starts afresh with a clean slate and a quiet mind.

Whips – Let's play 'Whack the pony'

The offering of whips like confectionaries, to riders of all ages who are barely able to hold their balance, let alone a whip, appears to be acceptable to many.

Armed and dangerous, they make futile attempts at kicking the horse to make him go, while they simultaneously interfere with his mouth in a vain attempt to smack his neck or bottom with the hand holding the whip. At the same time, the other hand pulls the opposite rein, unsuccessful in turning the horse in the wanted direction. The action results in confusing contradictory signals to the horse, with ensuing physical and emotional trauma.

The scenario is typical of many riding school riders. Leaders are unavailable to take the pressure off both horse and rider, leaving the rider void of her right to learn the correct basics of sitting on the horse. No time is given to the strengthening and build-up of the muscles in her legs in readiness for appropriate connections with the horse, which would eliminate the need for the whip.

It is often far easier to give a novice rider a whip to back up her kicking legs when coaching a class lesson!

Pass the parcel appears to be a common pastime at competitions; whips pass from one rider to another when she fails to convince her horse to go into the show ring!

Third party abuse of the horse is just as unforgivable as abuse directly from his rider.

You may think yourself to be a considerate user of the whip; do you tap your horse when he disobeys you, or as he reaches down for that juicy clump of grass when out hacking?

Even the slightest tap is abuse against the horse when not used solely for its purpose of reinforcing your inefficient leg connections. If you are proficient, the whip will be surplus to requirements.

It is my hope that further research on the sensitivity of the horse's skin will bring an end to the use of whips (and spurs). Meanwhile, if you insist on carrying a crop or a whip here is a guide in 'best practice' of the handling of both.

The short whip (crop)

The short whip can be a danger to the rider as much as to the horse; manufacturers will insist on attaching a wrist strap. I advise you to cut it off immediately. You should certainly not secure the whip strap around your wrist. The possible force caused by the horse's foot standing on the whip if you happen to take a fall could fracture your wrist.

The whip must only be used to encourage the horse a little more and to support your ineffective leg. As one rider may have need of a whip on a particular horse, you may be more effective and stronger through your leg connections and you don't require any artificial aids for the same horse.

It is **not** set in stone that you must use a whip when you reach a certain level of riding. However if you are a coach, you will be aware that riders in an Approved Pony Club Centre will be expected to be capable of carrying a short whip in either hand when taking their D+ Test.

Neither is it set in stone that the whip has to be used in conjunction with the inside leg only, though it will normally rest in your inside hand to back up your inside leg.

For instance, if your outside leg is not quite strong enough to perform a particular task, a light touch of the whip behind your leg on the same side will encourage him to move away from your leg and become a little lighter on that side.

However, the whip is never a substitute for legs, hands, or seat that has not been properly trained. When not in use, the whip should always be out of harm's way resting across your thigh.

If you intend to use a short whip to encourage the horse forward, you must:

■ Place your reins in the opposite hand to the one holding the whip. Your hand is then free to bring the whip just behind your leg to give the horse a sufficiently gentle tap to encourage him forward.

■ Never keep hold of the rein with the hand that is about to use the short whip behind your leg, because the pull on the rein as you bring your hand back will cause pain in the horse's mouth as well as bend him through his neck.

Changing the short whip over to the other hand

Following a change of rein, swap the whip over to your inside hand by doing the following:

■ Hold both reins with the hand already holding the whip.

■ With the palm of your opposite hand facing you, take hold of the top of the short whip with the thumb and index. Gently pull it up and out ensuring that as you take it over the horse's neck, you don't accidentally catch the horse with it. Secure the whip in your palm.

■ The whip should rest across your thigh until needed.

Sometimes, even a well-behaved horse will attempt an escape through his outside shoulder; if you are a competent rider don't be afraid to rest the whip against the horse's outside shoulder to encourage him to move away from the gentle pressure.

This use of the short whip can be invaluable when negotiating a course of jumps. However, a gross misconduct is its substitution of your lack of understanding why he felt it necessary to run out at a fence, or because of the incorrect use of your posture, weight, leg, and rein aids.

The long whip/schooling whip

The length of the whip enables you to use it effectively behind your leg without having to take your hands off the rein.

Changing the long whip over into the other hand is a little more complex than passing the short whip to the other hand. Because of its length, it would be necessary to lift your arm quite high to prevent the whip from catching the horse's shoulders, if you were to use the same method as with the short whip. I will explain it simply for you.

Let's say you want to change the whip over from the left hand to the right hand

■ Take both reins into the left hand.

■ Bring the right hand over towards the left hand by imagining you are holding a mug with no handle, and pouring water out of it so that the palm of your hand is facing the horse's ears.

■ Place your right hand below the left hand and cup your thumb around the underside of the whip.

■ The knuckle of the index finger of your right hand should rest beside the knuckle of the little finger of your left hand.

■ Fold the fingers of your right hand around the whip securing it with your palm.

■ Gently slide the whip out of your left hand; take it out a little to the left, and form an arch by bringing the whip back over the horse's withers to the right, being careful not to catch him with it.

- The tail of the whip should be uppermost as it forms the arch over the withers.

- Gently take the reins back in both hands and rest the whip over your right thigh.

Those shoes are hot!

Hoof protection was considered a necessary evil right from the beginning of the domestication of the horse.

The maximum hoof and leg trauma he suffered in his natural habitat was probably when fleeing a predator. The horse's legs and feet were now exposed to trauma from varying terrains when carrying his rider into battle, or pulling heavy loads and so on. Without protection, his hooves would deteriorate and become sore. His unfitness for work would cause suffering for both horse and owner.

Shoes evolved from simple leather hide boots and other natural materials to the common shoes of today with nails hammered through their holes into the wall of the hoof. I wonder how many nails through time hit the sensitive parts of the hoof before someone realised why the horse was lame.

Memories - as a youngster and into my teens - bring back the sounds of the clippety clop of the shoe iron. However, some of the ponies I rode were often barefoot, though I think for reasons other than the owner's conscience. However, I don't recall any of them suffering from major ailments of the hoof.

Although sensing a negative emotion when having my own horses shod over the years, but being uncertain of the consequences of not shoeing, I felt I must conform.

I am in no position to give advice on this subject because it is a reasonably recent enlightenment for me. Nevertheless, I can vouch for the success of correct management of barefoot horses, having spent time with those that happily reside in the respectful care of two of my good friends.

The long held traditional beliefs of the horse being incapable of doing the work he does without the wearing of shoes is now exposed as fallacy and abuse, thanks to technology that is finally able to prove its point.

There is a great deal of evidence that proves the negative effects of shoeing, not only in deformity and degenerative conditions of the hoof such as navicular disease, but the appearance of splints, back problems, ligament injuries and much more.

My goal on this subject is to illuminate your conscience into looking into the option of barefoot trimming.

10

Redeeming saviours

Here, at the pinnacle, the substance of the preceding chapters amalgamates effortlessly. The author takes pride in fetching you to the point of total trust and a willingness to take the last leap of faith in replacing *all* the **aids** with small segments of **connections**. For example, rather than using the seat, legs and hands in one fell swoop and blocking the horse from all angles, you will offer the horse a little at a time, perfecting each segment before offering the next. The newly awakened and nurtured power of your positive energy oozes, enhancing the feel and synchronisation between you and the horse. His footfalls become easy to feel; rhythm, tempo and speed are absorbed easily in your mind; you are now able to concentrate on your own posture instead of keeping the horse moving. The instilled traditional **aid** sequences and artillery are now fading as you build up a whole new set of connections. The most striking outcome of the process is the beautiful, trusting relationship between you and your horse.

The camera never lies!

The camera, a vital piece of equipment as a truth teller, is an essential part of your toolbox.

It is imperative, that as you convert the contents of this guide into physical practices, you have clear evidence for candid analysing of each aspect in its entirety. Photo and film documentation will enlighten you to the slightest anomaly, for example:

- When checking the horse for uneven muscle mass. It can sometimes be difficult to come to unwavering conclusions with the naked eye alone.

- The camera is invaluable in documenting your riding technique. Have someone film you and the horse when in the saddle, from all angles. On playback, make a note of your various body, leg and hand positions, and any lop-sidedness. Placing a ruler over your body parts in a photo, such as across the back of your shoulders, or vertically to view your ear, hip, heel line will confirm any deviances.

- Make a note of the horse's simultaneous response behaviours and check them against the checklists in the guide. A swish of the tail when ridden is usually a clear indication of some discomfort.

- The photo/video will open your eyes to the stance and engagement of your horse. What you may feel as **acceptance of the bit,** the camera may truthfully challenge; your horse may be on his forehand.

- Place the ruler on the photo, horizontally across the top of the poll, which should be the highest point. Does the ruler confirm this, or does it reveal part of the horse's neck as the highest point?

- Place the ruler vertically on the head of the horse to determine if he is on, in front of, or behind the vertical. The latter is **not** recommended. If the poll is not at the highest point, you will likely find that the horse's head is behind the vertical.

■ If your horse refuses or cat leaps fences, and the photo reveals a horse that is hollow through his back with his head high, and ears startlingly upright or back, the **truth teller** has supplied you with the reason for his **disobedience!**

The above list is only a taster of the information you can gain and learn from the camera, and of course the **ruler!** However, it will open doors into your continued learning and a much-improved relationship with your horse.

■ By enlarging images, you will see more clearly, the good and the not so good elements.

If you are open to admitting to your own faults, and willing to try out the exercises on the following pages, I guarantee that vast improvements *will* follow.

Some of the exercises may go against the grain of 'proper teaching methods', but go with it and you will see and feel improvements in both you and your horse.

Once again, have someone document the evidence on camera. Make comparisons with the initial filming evidence and notice the positive differences.

Connecting through positive energy, your seat, weight, and legs

The term **connection** means **joining, fitting together, linking, and association.** However, it conjures up an altogether diverse thought, feeling, and vision when riding the horse. Connecting with the horse while using your thought and imagination allows your combined energies to work together, eliminating many of the pressures caused by the **natural aids**.

Connection is the term I encourage rather than **aid**, and one that I adopt in my own coaching and riding practices. I urge you to give it a go. Your entire way of riding will transform, as **connections** with your horse will cause your mind to invoke completely different images to the ones that currently manifest as you give your **aids.**

The simpler you keep the **connections**, the better the outcome. Always remember the phrase *Less is more.*

Crucially, don't push or press down with each seat bone; to do so would cause the horse to hollow due to the pressure and discomfort.

You will offer your horse complete freedom as you each mirror the other with ease; you will balance over his centre, with your legs naturally and softly placed underneath your body.

A gentle caress of your seat when asking for forward movement, or a simple shift in your weight, becomes very effective in guiding direction or a particular shape. It is about communicating with him and nothing more.

Positive energy

Everything and everyone on this planet is the creation of the same universal energy. How you feel emotionally or physically will dictate the positivity or negativity of your energy, which is detected in your aura - the energy that extends from your body and surrounds you.

Sometimes, when our energy fields collide, we feel an electric shock! We can sense a person's negative energy by the uncomfortable feeling we get when a particular person gets too close to our energy field. Sometimes we feel goose bumps or the hairs on the back of our necks standing on end.

If you approach a horse while feeling at odds with the world, he will instantly notice your negative energy and he **won't** want to be near you.

On the other hand, he will relish the positive energy oozing from your aura. Horses can't get enough of our positive energy, particularly when they are suffering emotionally. It has an enormous calming influence on them and a sense of wellbeing.

■ Visualise, if you can, a beam of golden light relentlessly flowing down from the sky into the top of your head. Feel it flow warmly down through every part of your head, body, arms, and legs, through your feet, and into the earth, all the while feeling the sense of a warm glow. Using this imagery when in the saddle will result in softly flowing **connections** and a quietly flowing horse. It is certainly an asset when we constantly bombard our horses' auras with what is quite often negative energy.

If you don't feel or see the energy flow, don't worry or concentrate on the fact. Simply say, *"Positive energy is flowing down through my head, body, legs and feet, and into the earth"*. The **intent** will be enough to get it flowing.

Riding with energy

True riding – if there is such a thing - is not about the submission of the horse through manipulation of our artillery the second our seat hits the saddle. It is about respecting his dignity and forming an alliance of energies. I know first-hand how our energy, backed up with positive breath, thought, imagination, visualisation and his trust, blows traditional beliefs and teachings out of the water when it comes to being at one with the horse.

The human instinct is to push ourselves to be the best. Sadly, there often appears to be no distinction in whether our energy is focused on the manipulation of an inanimate object, or a live animal; the human drive is the same. The energy force is tremendous and frequently aggressive. Its transference to the horse is often negative - such a pity.

The positive influence of the horse is your goal. Knowing which foot is on the ground and when, is important. Applying your leg connection when the foot is about to leave the ground, will encourage the horse to use his hind leg on that side to drive himself forward.

If his foot is off the ground when a leg connection is given, the horse will increase the elevation of his leg.

The progressive trialling of mini connections, with the use of various seat, leg and body positions, and the varying degrees of pressure caused by your connections, will also heighten the sensitivity of your energy, mind, and body as they begin to gel with the horse. There is no rollercoaster effect as you throw all your artillery at the horse in one go; it is just you and him, each giving, little by little, with much faster progress and longevity than you will realise.

You must know the footfall sequence for all the horse's manoeuvers so that you can correctly ask the horse to place his feet.

- Before, and when getting back in the saddle, visualise your energy flowing strongly through you.

- Encourage the horse to walk forward while you allow yourself a little time to simply be in the present moment; feel his movement, as if your bodies entwine in harmony. Let your positive energy flow from your body to his and feel it build.

- Feel that your core is strong and flowing.

- Allow everything around you to disappear as you become at one with your horse. You now feel confident in gently asking him for more engagement and energy, by putting a little more swing into the natural hip movement as you feel the energy flow down through your thighs.

- Don't allow your body to lean to the side; imagine a disconnection of your hips from your upper body; they belong to your legs.

- Despite being told that you must always ride from the inside leg to the outside rein, I suggest that you have no contact at all for now. The horse will not fall over; he is quite capable of maintaining his balance if you strive to keep your own.

- As one leg connects, don't block the horse by putting your opposite leg on his belly. In fact, take that leg away completely for now. Feel your horse really begin to move more freely. Swap legs, ensuring your opposite leg doesn't interfere.

- As an experiment, put your opposite leg back on his belly; watch and feel how he may begin to crumble due to the small but dramatic restriction. Then feel and watch how he will work willingly for you as you remove your leg.

- With practice, the variations of your leg placement and pressure will finally find their sanctuary, whether your leg is simply asking the horse for more engagement, or you want him to move away, or you are asking him to bend around your leg. You have the beginnings of lateral movement!

Remember, you are learning to use yourself correctly, not merely learning how to use the 'aids'. Be aware that what works for one horse, may not work for another. If you ride various horses, compromise may be necessary to suit each horse. It may seem tedious to begin with, but you must listen to the individual and adapt accordingly. The upside is that you will have an array of positive tools up your sleeve to mix and match effortlessly!

Feeling and synchronising with the horse's motion

You may have heard the term **feeling and following the motion**. I prefer the term **feeling and synchronising** *with* **the motion** because the term **following** conjures up pictures of the rider being behind the motion of the horse, waiting for him to react to a connection and the rider then following. The term **synchronise** means **working together in unison**.

When you are generally relaxed and allowing through your hips and pelvis, you will feel that each of your hips mirrors those of the horse as he brings each hind leg underneath him to propel himself forward. You must be sensitive to the motion if you are to use your leg connections at the opportune moment; for example, when asking for more engagement of a hind leg or asking the horse to move diagonally.

- As the horse steps onto his **right hind foot** in the four beat walk, his **right hip lifts**, at the same time lifting your **right hip forward and up**.

- As his **right foot** then leaves the ground, your **hip on the same side** drops backwards and down as you feel **his hip** do the same.

- Your hip movement follows exactly, the forward, up, backward, down motion of the horse's right hip during the process, which is just like backpedalling a bicycle.

- As the horse then **steps onto his left hind foot**, your **left hip** will mirror his **left hip**.

- As each hip drops, the horse's barrel also swings out of the way of the foot that is about to leave the ground; the barrel will **swing to the left** as the horse's **right foot** leaves the ground.

- You will feel the movement easily if you are balanced and soft through your pelvis.

■ Ask someone to stand behind the horse and tell you each time his **inside hind foot** touches the ground. As it does, be conscious of **your hip on the same side** lifting in unison with the **horse's hip**, because **the instant his foot rises and your hip begins its downward motion, is the precise moment to positively influence the engagement and direction of his leg.** Your thigh and leg need only mimic the swing of his barrel with the smallest amount of pressure.

Before you mount up, watch the horse's movement as he is led away from you in a straight line with the stirrups hanging down. Take notice of how, **when a hind foot touches the ground, the corresponding hip lifts.** As the **same foot leaves the ground, the hip drops, and his belly swings out of the way.** The hanging stirrups will give the vision more clarity.

Substitute your horse for a stool; practice the motion. Softly, sit upright, lower back naturally arched. Thighs parallel to the floor; feet hip width apart as they sit securely on the ground. Begin to perfect the art of backpedalling until:

■ You feel the soft, smooth continuous forward, up, backward, down movement of each hip, as each seat bone, surrounded by the imaginary softest cotton wool, simply dusts the seat as it freely travels around its circle.

■ You can balance with ease from your head to your feet.

■ Your upper body freely turns around independently of your pelvis.

Be aware of how your body reacts throughout.

■ Do you feel any tension, imbalance, or discomfort?

■ Feeling the swing of the horse's back will be problematic if you grip with your thighs.

■ The horse will have limited freedom to do your bidding if you are unbalanced, stiff in any area, and not allowing or soft through your pelvis when in the saddle.

■ The blocking of his sides by your stiff legs will inhibit his strides.

■ He will mirror your stiffness.

■ The horse will suffer the feeling of a blow to his barrel with a plank as it collides with your lower leg on its return, if you delay your thigh and leg action, rather than the flowing togetherness in the same direction.

■ As your hips flow left and right, be aware that your weight remains equal along your pelvis. Uneven pressure will restrict the horse's forward movement. Allow the flow of energy to equalise you physically and mentally.

■ Split the full rotation into smaller manageable segments; for instance, practice sliding one seat bone back and forth until it becomes second nature, with no negatives. Then add another element of the process and so on.

■ The mastery of each segment will allow for its complete reintegration in building a solid foundation. Always simplify any process by breaking it down into easy manageable pieces.

After all, a driving instructor wouldn't ask a first time driver to turn on the engine, put her foot on the pedal and drive from A to B. It is first necessary to find your way around the controls without the engine running, then adding on the pieces bit by bit to build a solid foundation, and so secure the desired outcome.

Feeling the horse's movement at the trot is a little more difficult because there is a moment of suspension in the two beat movement. There is also the tendency to bounce around in the saddle if you are unbalanced and tense. Ensure you are capable of sitting to the trot before attempting this. Lunge lessons are an ideal way of leaving you free to concentrate on your balance issues.

Assuming you are adept at sitting to the trot, you will now influence the horse in the same way as when in the walk.

Gently push the horse into the trot with a little more exaggeration of your hip motion and a gentle caress of your lower leg. It is crucial that you stay in harmony with the horse and your hips stay in the constant rhythm.

- As your hips continue to flow in harmony and rhythm with the horse's hips, picture the horse now trotting. Your hips and lower legs will do most of the work for you.

- Don't dwell on any failures; bring yourself into the present moment again. Breathe in deeply and, as you exhale, imagine your hips naturally swinging in a positive rhythm in harmony with the horse as he complies with the gentle pressures of your seat and lower leg. Ask for short gentle bursts of trot until you are able to maintain longer bouts with a soft swinging seat.

- If the horse loses momentum in the trot, his motion will be more subtle; your hips may not have the natural rhythmic swing created by him. Gently, with energy flowing through both legs, caress his sides simultaneously to re-establish the required pace.

- Now revert to using each leg independently, to influence the horse in lifting each hind leg higher and further underneath him, and to help him propel himself forward, rather than pushing himself forward with his hind legs. See in your mind's eye the energy in your legs connecting and flowing through the horse's legs, and feel the effortless effects. Do **not** place constant undue pressure on his sides causing him to ignore you.

■ Principally, you must know where each of the horse's four legs is at any moment in each gait. When practicing the above exercise with a calm mind, relaxed body and being in the present moment, you will begin to feel the full sequence of each leg movement.

■ Close your eyes if it is safe to do so; it will heighten your sense of touch and hearing. You will begin to feel and hear the sound of each hind and front hoof throughout the cycle, from touch down to touch down.

The sequence of footfalls

The horse plays the leading role in the art of **learning to ride**. However, that role is often undermined. Riders and teachers take it for granted that his presence is all that is required. **He is merely a tool of the trade**. How the horse uses his legs in the various gaits appears to bear no importance to the teacher until much later on in the pupil's riding career, if at all. The pupil then passes her knowledge down to the next innocent rider.

Riders also fail to recognise the difference between the horse's steps and his strides.

■ A step is counted as each leg steps.

■ A stride is the completion of the full sequence of steps, whether it is in walk, trot, or canter; the count begins when one particular hoof hits the ground each time.

■ The power of each gait is produced in the hindquarters and driven by the hind legs.

All riders, no matter how inexperienced, should learn from the outset the following list of footfalls.

The walk

■ There are four steps to one stride (four time beat). Count 1-2-3-4 as you feel each beat.

■ The sequence of footfalls to the walk, for example: the right hind followed by the right fore, then the left hind followed by the left fore.

■ The push of the horse's hind foot as he drives his body forward forces the front foot on the same side to step forward for two reasons:

- to prevent an obstruction as the hind foot steps into its path, and

- to re-instate the horse's balance.

■ He may appear to start his stride with the stepping out of his front foot, because his hind foot has not yet actually left the ground. If the hind foot was to leave the ground before the front foot escaped, a collision of both could result in injury.

The trot

■ There are two steps to this diagonal stride (two time). Count 1-2-1-2 as each diagonal pair of legs hits the ground in a constant rhythm.

■ The sequence of footfalls to the trot, for example is the right hind leg and left foreleg together, with a moment of suspension, then the left hind leg and right foreleg together with a moment of suspension.

■ The horse doesn't need to make major balancing motions with his head and neck when trotting; they remain relatively still.

The canter

- A three beat stride followed by a moment of suspension. A horse may canter on an incorrect lead; he may become disunited due to rider imbalance. Count 1-2-3- in a constant rhythm with each footfall.

- The sequence of footfalls for left lead canter is: the right hind, followed with left hind and right foreleg together, followed by the left foreleg, with a moment of suspension.

- The right hind begins the sequence with a short push of the horse's foot.

- As the pair of legs in the next footfall takes over, the **left hind extends** while **the right foreleg covers less ground**.

- The stride completes as the **left front foot** touches down on a long stride.

The rein back

- The rein back uses the same diagonal pairs of legs as in the trot.

Rhythm

Rhythm is the beat of the sequence of footfalls within each stride, described above.

The horse has a rhythm that is natural to the individual; it may be perfect, it may be flawed depending on factors including physical and emotional problems, laziness, or a highly-strung horse. Fully investigate any flaws.

The ultimate goal is to allow the horse to show off the same innate rhythmic and elegant ability that he has at liberty.

Feeling and synchronising with the horse will actually make him think that the idea to work with you this way was his! He will thank you for giving him the choice.

Tempo

Defined as the speed of the rhythm of the footfalls within each gait, the tempo refers to the frequency of the completed stride per minute.

Any changes to the length of the stride, such as from working trot to medium trot, should not affect a change in tempo; the horse simply covers more ground.

Speed

Often mistaken for tempo, the speed refers to how fast the horse is moving; for example, the walk is slow, the trot is faster. The horse's stride may not lengthen as he makes the transition into trot; he covers more ground due to the speed.

The horse's temperament must be a consideration when working with rhythm, tempo, and speed. Your decisions will affect his movement and his state of mind.

Riding to music is an extremely effective and stress busting way to find and maintain rhythm. However, finding the right piece of music with the ideal tempo can sometimes be difficult. You wouldn't use a powerful piece with a slow tempo for a Shetland pony, or music with a fast diddly diddly dee tempo, for a tall long striding dressage horse!

So, without further ado, I introduce to you…

Humpty Dumpty!

Don't knock it until you have given it a go! It eliminates all tension and a serious attitude. It may be the very tip of the iceberg training tool, but its simplicity and effective results will keep you and the horse entertained and interested.

This nursery rhyme, with its constant rhythm and simple tempo change, is an ideal accessory in accomplishing rhythm by a rider of any age. Children enjoy Humpty Dumpty; adults are embarrassed at the thought! However, when tested, it remains a part of their toolbox, along with other suitable rhythmic tunes which work just as well; for now, Humpty Dumpty suits the example.

Why Humpty Dumpty?

■ Its very existence eliminates the need for overuse of your seat and legs when asking for impulsion, and the need to pull on the reins to slow the horse down. **(Are you aware, that pulling on the reins does *not* slow a horse? He will usually speed up in an attempt to escape the pain of the pull).**

■ Instruction is often wrongly aimed at the rider's encouragement of the horse into a rhythm; it is impossible for him to find a rhythm if the rider is constantly in conflict. If the horse is not moving forward in a rhythm, the emphasis is often placed on his non-compliance, because the fault of the rider goes unseen. Any tuition must be geared towards increasing rider ability, so that you naturally influence the horse; it is wrong to gear it towards your manipulation of him.

■ With this simple rhyme, you have the freedom to focus on uttering in rhythm to help maintain your rhythm in any pace. You choose the tempo, being careful not to push the horse out of his natural movement. This, along with your power of thought, calm deep breathing, and the rest of your toolkit, will allow the horse to work with you with impulsion, rhythm, and tempo.

Try this exercise in the walk

■ As the rhythm ticks in your head, allow your body to synchronise with it. In turn, the horse will synchronise with your body motion. Be careful not to push him from his natural rhythm.

■ Increase the tempo a little and feel the result! Slow it down while keeping up the impulsion and the rhythm; feel the positive result.

■ The horse may try to manipulate your body into making a return to a rhythm he likes to use when chilling in the field that you might find difficult to ignore to begin with. Don't fight with him; simply maintain the regularity in your head and he will come around to your way.

The temptation to stay with the motion of a horse that thinks you are incapable of making him work, rather than asking him to work with your motion will lessen the more you practice. He will soon realise you are not the pushover he thought you were! Obviously, you fully investigated the reason for his laziness prior to concluding that he is simply being cheeky – didn't you?

■ The sound of your soft but positive voice will ensure your continuous breathing.

■ Picture the horse working with you in harmony. However, don't let your mind wander; he will take control of it in an instant.

■ Listen, and reply positively to any negative reaction he shows.

If you have not heard of the rhyme, it goes like this:

Humpty Dumpty sat on a wall,
Humpty Dumpty had a great fall.
All the king's horses and all the king's men,
couldn't put Humpty together again.

Walking a straight line

Insufficient emphasis is often given to learning to ride a straight line in the lower levels of riding. Riders are in a hurry to get into trot because **walking is boring** and their teachers are all too often happy to oblige. The horses are none too happy either, dragged in complete disorder because the rider is unable to ask him to walk straight ahead.

With regular practice of the previous exercises, asking your horse to walk in a straight line and maintaining it will be a **walk in the park!**

- ■ Don't concentrate on trying to achieve a perfect track. Use your imagery, breath, energy - all the tools at your disposal.

- ■ Take your legs away from the saddle, bend your knees and bring them up slightly, feeling equal weight down both sides of your torso. If the horse was not walking a straight line before you lifted your legs, he will now! What does that tell you?

- ■ Gently and gradually, begin to place your legs back in their correct position. The moment you feel or see any negative reaction, be aware of why the horse has reacted at that very moment. Is your leg stiff? Do you have a problem with a particular part of your leg? Ask an experienced person to check your position and help you to correct it. **If you are crooked, none of your connections will work. If the horse is crooked, he will struggle to walk on a straight line.**

■ Use props such as ground poles; lay out cones with a runway effect to help you. Use your imagination and helpers.

You will find the above much more useful rather than constantly being told to use your **aids.**

Stopping - brains not brawn

Asking the horse to slow down or to stop is so simple whilst using the minimum gentle resistance. Yet so many riders use such brute force and then wonder why the horse doesn't do as **he is told!**

Effecting the slow down or halt must come from the hindquarters. The reins are merely a gate that is **closed** to initiate a stop, or **ajar** to allow the continued forward movement of the horse. Of course, if your horse is sensitive to the correctness of your seat and legs, you may need no rein at all when practicing with the individual segments of the connection.

The connections to halt

■ Imagine the horse's body as a tube of toothpaste. Push the paste gently up through the tube towards the loosened cap (your hands) as you close your lower legs around the horse to keep him moving forward.

■ As the paste nears the cap, grow tall as you lift your chest up and out slightly, which will move your shoulders back. You will feel your back naturally **brace;** your pelvis will tilt backwards very slightly, shifting your point of gravity. The shift of your pelvis will very gently bring your inner thighs closer to the saddle and lighten your seat, which will encourage the horse to slow down.

■ Your legs continue their encouragement of the horse in bringing his hind legs underneath him.

- As you feel the energy beginning to fill the neck of the tube, simply sit still, while your legs remain on the horse's sides.

- Your elbows sit passively by your waist as your hands no longer follow the nod of the horse's head. Usually, the resistance he feels from the still rein is enough for him to halt. Because you want to prevent the paste oozing from the opening, the effect will be a very light resisting rein.

- The moment the horse responds is the same moment you must reward him by releasing the pressure.

- Maintain the rhythm until the horse stops.

- If he doesn't halt, gently close your fingers around the rein, with a following gentle give. If the horse still resists the rein and doesn't stop, it will most likely be due to tension in your body or hands.

- Abandon the exercise; ask the horse to walk on. Once your mind is relaxed and calm, ride through the procedure again.

Implant the following phrase into your mind; it will remind you to handle the reins delicately when asking of the horse with the outside rein:

I take, you give, I give.

The half halt is not rocket science

The half halt appears to be a mystery to many riders. Maybe it would be easier to perform if you imagined it in its correct term, the **re-balancer**. What image does the term **half halt** manifest in your mind? A horse stopped by the rein maybe?

Now think of the term **re-balance**. Do you now see an image of the horse permitted to engage his hindquarters and lighten his forehand?

As you received an image of each 'term' you will also have felt a reaction in your solar plexus, particularly if the half halt daunts you.

Think of them again, this time being conscious of the feeling you get. Ok, I think we will agree that the image of the half halt may cause you to block the horse in front.

On the other hand, harmony prevails in your imagery if you allow the horse to **re-balance** himself with a little **rebalancing** of your own body. So, from now on, I will use the term **re-balancer**; after all, the horse must **re-balance** himself in preparation for a change of pace, school movement, or simply if he just needs to **re-balance** himself. He can only do this if you are completely balanced.

The re-balancing process is the same method as for the halt above, with one difference; at the very last second (but with preparation), as the horse slows down to the halt, **you change your mind!** There you go, what could be simpler. Rather than riding the horse up into the closed toothpaste tube cap that prevents the paste from oozing out, you purely unscrew the cap as necessary. It must be unscrewed carefully. To open the cap too fast would result in the horse losing the balance he has managed to maintain up to now.

Follow the procedure for the halt until you reach the part that begins **As you feel the energy beginning to fill the neck of the toothpaste tube, sit still while your legs remain on the horse's sides....** Now follow the process below.

■ Just before the toothpaste reaches the cap, the horse will feel lighter; you will then feel the slight resistance in the rein. At that point say to yourself, with a time span of four seconds, *"I've-changed-my-mind"*. At the same time, **connect-with-your-legs**, **release-with-the-rein**. See it flow gently in your imagery.

■ Remember to maintain your leg connections as you sit back down into your seat and ask for the forward movement, allowing for the continuous flow.

■ Continue to repeat Humpty Dumpty throughout the whole sequence to ensure the constant flow of energy, rhythm, tempo, and balance.

■ Use the re-balancer imagery frequently. Be sure to bring it into play before any change.

Implant the following phrase into your mind:

The upper leg means slow,
the lower leg means go;
Both together mean shorter steps.

Up the Pace - time to have some fun!

The transition to rising trot

■ Maintain the impulsion whilst feeling the swing of your hips and the horse's footfalls.

■ Without altering Humpty Dumpty's rhythm and tempo, imagine you are now making the transition to rising trot; let the toothpaste ooze just enough to help the horse into the smoothest transition through your leg connections.

■ Think only of the constant tempo in your head as your seat leaves, and again makes contact with the saddle. Any loss of rhythm will result in a loss of connection and synchronisation between you and the horse.

■ Remain sitting until you feel your **outside hip** lift. Simultaneously, as it lifts, the horse will begin the rising trot sequence by **pushing you out of the saddle** as he trots with each diagonal pair of legs. You **simply assist the**

push with your own gentle but energetic effort. You will then ride the trot on the correct diagonal pair of legs. A full explanation of riding on the correct diagonal pair of legs is given below.

When rising from the saddle, your body doesn't rise and fall straight up and down. Picture your upper body gently sloping in the direction of an escalator: more forwards, then down. Your back should remain flat as you bring your body forward from the hip joints and carry your shoulders above your knees. Your belly button must move towards the horse's ears.

Ride down the long side of the arena mouthing *"Humpty Dumpty..."* As you reach the corner, maintain the same tempo. Remember to **re-balance** before the corner to ensure a smooth flowing movement. Feel how the horse keeps his momentum as he trots through the corner.

- Now practice keeping the rhythm while changing the tempo. Ride to the next corner; just before the turn, begin to slow the tempo of the rhythm. You will need to maintain an active **rise**. Its energy will ensure the horse's momentum as the tempo of his trot mirrors the same in your body. Your body will react to the change of the beat in your mind.

- Practice riding around the arena, changing the tempo of the rhythm up and down.

- Feel as the horse begins to react to your request with more willingness as he settles into your energy.

- Ride over ground poles at their correct set distances for the stride of your horse, towards, over, and away from them, while voicing the rhythm. Notice how the horse maintains energy, rhythm and balance through the process instead of losing it as he negotiates the poles.

■ The energy you feel as the horse lifts his legs over the poles, should be as constant without the use of poles.

Flow from trot to canter and canter to trot

■ **Ensure a flowing transition from the trot**: maintain the current tempo by continuing to sing **Humpty Dumpty** as you gently take your seated position, and make the connection into the three beat canter. Imagine the picture of the perfect canter in your head; practice the exercises as for the trot.

■ **Ensure a flowing transition to the trot:** in asking for the transition from the canter to the trot, picture a soft flowing movement while you maintain the tempo – physically and vocally; remain in your saddle for a few strides until you can clearly feel the lifting of your **outside hip**. Then simply assist the horse as he gently pushes your seat from the saddle, enabling you to sit on the correct diagonal pair of legs.

The importance of riding on the correct diagonal in the rising trot

Sitting on the correct diagonal: your seat is in the saddle when the horse's **outside foreleg** and **inside hind** leg are on the ground.

Some consider the importance of sitting on the correct diagonal when on a straight line negligible. Teachers sometimes tend to ignore the fact that a rider may be sitting on the **inside** diagonal.

Nonetheless, it is **crucial** that the horse's muscles are worked equally on both sides. If you ride on a favoured diagonal for any length of time, the horse will become weak on his opposite side; he will be incapable of working freely.

When out hacking, a **frequent change** of diagonal is essential to prevent the horse becoming stiff and weaker on one side of his body.

*You must change your diagonal
with every rein change.*

Circling and turning – which diagonal?

When circling or turning, the outside of the horse lengthens as his inside shortens. The **outside hind leg** must therefore make more of an extended effort to keep up with the inside leg in getting round the circle.

However, the **inside hind leg** must step further underneath the horse's belly to keep him on the correct track whilst maintaining the correct bend through his body, *and* bearing the bulk of your weight and his.

By rising, and taking some of your weight off the horse's back at the moment his **inside hind leg** and his **outside foreleg** leave the ground and enter their moment of suspension, you will not inhibit the movement, nor destabilise his balance. The horse is then free to make the necessary adjustments to his stride.

You then sit as the same diagonal pair of legs hits the ground, having done their job without any interference from your seat.

You may also find that your inside leg is steadier than if you were to rise on the opposite diagonal.

A commonly used explanation of how to sit on the correct diagonal in the rising trot involves rising from the saddle as the outside shoulder moves away from you; you sit as the same shoulder comes back towards you. It may be the only example of which you are familiar.

You sit on the horse's **outside diagonal** pair of legs. You may also be advised to **rise and fall with the foot on the wall**.

Glancing at the outside shoulder to determine when it is moving forward and backward can be difficult. You could chalk on the shoulder to make the shoulder movement clearer. Does it make it clearer for you, or does it remain as clear as mud?

Let me make it simple for you!

A far better way to feel the correct timing is to use your newfound skills of feeling and synchronising with the horse's movement, as in the alternative method below. With practice, you will feel the horse's lateral two-time movement of the trot: **as you feel each of your hips rise, the horse is pushing off with the hind foot on the same side.**

Unfortunately, if you haven't been taught to ride in harmony with your horse by feeling and synchronising, you will find the example below difficult.

The left rein example:

- At the very moment your **right hip** rises, the horse's **outside hind foot** and **inside fore (left diagonal)** have touched down in readiness to thrust his body forward, while his opposite diagonal pair, **the inside hind foot** and the **outside fore (right diagonal)** have just left the ground and are approaching their moment of suspension. Now is the time to rise from your saddle.

- When you are at the highest point of your rise, the **inside hind leg**, working in unison with the **outside foreleg (right diagonal)** has freely stepped up underneath the horse's body, and is now approaching the ground.

- Your seat sits in the saddle at the same time that the horse's **right diagonal** pair of legs meets the ground.

Learning to 'feel' your diagonals instead of looking at the horse's shoulder will be difficult *only* if you are unable to feel and synchronise with the horse at the walk. Once it feels natural to you, a whole new realm of being at one with your horse rather than being merely familiar with his shoulder, will be open to you!

A **grass roots** client - an eight-year-old girl named Millie - knows where each of her pony's legs is at any one moment.

A one-time explanation two days ago on how and why to ride on the correct trotting diagonal, resulted in perfection each time Abi the pony made the transition from walk to trot on a particular rein. There was no unbalancing of pony and rider while searching for the shoulder movement, just a natural shift of the rider's seat from the saddle at the opportune moment. The positive change in the pony's movement and balance raised the bar considerably.

In spite of Abi's on-going emotional healing process from past rider abuse, Millie uses minimal connections from her toolbox, yet receives outstanding results!

Look, no hands!

Often, the rider's initial reaction is to grab the reins when a horse appears to be going too fast in any pace. The horse pulls back against the rider and so a fight begins, both becoming more agitated and tense. The horse will **not** slow down!

However, he *will* slow down if the rider is brave enough to ease off the contact and slow her rise down as she slowly affirms vocally and respiratory.

Repeating the phrase, *Slow-my-rise-down*, works extremely well. You have to trust that he will listen to your breathing and the steadiness of your movement. You can begin to put your own phrases to the pictures in your mind of the results you require of any aspect.

Sometimes, stress inflicted by his rider will cause the horse's mind to spiral from a level of a slight gesture that something is wrong, to a level where he literally flees for his life.

At this stage, all the tools in your bag will most likely fall to the ground where you can't reach them.

Therefore, you are also likely to begin your pull of the reins. It is blatant abuse to allow a horse to reach the stage of being in a blind panic.

Have you heard the phrase, *the horse galloped off in a blind panic*? A galloping horse has difficulty focusing. He must rely on you to keep him safe. A fleeing, galloping horse does **not** see the hazards ahead of him, hence the phrase.

Revelation; you have the ability to lower your horse's mind from a state of high anxiety to a peaceful state of mind – not merely relaxed, but **peaceful**. You also have the ability to **maintain** his peaceful mind. The only tools you need are the desire, your own quiet mind, and your time and patience.

- Imagine the state of your mind on a scale of 1 to 10; 1 being very calm and 10 being through the roof. Bring a memory of an incident that raised your mind over number 5 on the scale. How long did it take you to calm down? Who got the sharp end of your tongue before you came back down to earth?

- Now imagine your horse's mind on the same scale. A scale of 2 is a calm horse, excellent for a good working relationship; 5 is beginning to tip over the point of no return, and 7 is past the point of no return. Your mind must be in a non-thinking state if you are to keep your horse happy and contented. Imagine how peaceful he would be if your mind was so quiet that he was able to lower his head and close his eyes – WOW!!

> **Having journeyed with me to this point I feel it is now pertinent to offer you my second gift. It is precious. I know your growing open-mindedness will allow you to use it wisely and effectively.**

It is the gift of power in helping your horse through traumatic events, or even simply helping him to be peaceful.

Try the following when you are alone with your horse, and he is resting.

- Stand passively by him, far enough away so that he is unable to touch and distract you. Every part of you is relaxed and still as your mind remains in the here and now with your physical body. In turn, your breathing and heart rate will work at their natural capacity.

- Softly **focus** your eyes on a static object while keeping all intent on the horse.

- Now gently rub the thumb and index finger of one or both hands together; it will help to stop you from thinking. If you are sceptical, do the exercise and try to think about what you have planned for tomorrow. You will find it difficult to think, because you are focusing on being in the present moment rather than on tomorrow!

- Thoughts will probably come into your mind to begin with. Simply acknowledge them, imagine surrounding them in a bubble and allowing them to float away. Don't dwell on them.

- Noises will simply disappear if you treat them in the same way. However, for example, if you hear noises in the next stable and you think *"What is that horse doing?"* all kinds of thoughts and pictures will gush into your mind to distract you. Gremlins that live in our conscious minds are very good at sabotaging our attempts to be in the present moment. They feed off our negative thoughts because they can't survive without them.

- Imagine a plain white board in your mind's eye. The aim is to keep it white. If you find anything appearing on the board such as writing, pictures, or even voices, acknowledge them, then simply wipe the board clean. Don't think about what you see, just wipe them away while maintaining your soft breathing. It is ok to have thoughts drifting through, just don't let them stay. Acknowledge them and let them pass.

- As your mind becomes quieter, the horse's mind will follow. You will notice how he becomes more relaxed, his head will drop, his eyes will start to droop, his bottom lip will relax, and his breathing will become deep and peaceful. He may pass wind, he will yawn, he may wander around his stable for a while looking for a comfortable place. He may start scratching himself.

- He may try to distract you with a nuzzle of his nose. If a horse is not used to the kind of peaceful energy you are giving him, he may feel a little uncomfortable. If this happens, bring yourself out of your present state for a few seconds until he settles down, and then begin again.

- The effects of this beautiful energy are accumulative. The more you link into your horse this way, the more profound his wellbeing will be. Meanwhile your wellbeing and peaceful mind will become normal to you. People will comment on the change in your whole demeanour! You will see and feel the enormous changes occurring in every aspect of your relationship with your horse and your life as a whole.

- Remember, the horse's mind will always mirror yours with no exceptions!

Improve your ability at the canter

The canter is the only gait with a rocking motion as well as up and down. To improve at the canter, you must know how the movement affects your seat and balance, because any deviation from correctness will have an adverse effect on the horse's movement and balance.

When the horse is in left lead canter, he leads with his left front leg; however, the sequence given below begins with the pushing off with the **right hind** leg.

■ First, the horse coils his back under him, bringing his back legs under his body.

■ He puts his **right hind** leg to the floor first and thrusts himself forward. As he does so, his weight goes back onto his **right hip**, lifting the front of his body, his head, and his neck.

■ The thrust from his **right hind** leg rolls him onto his **left hind** leg and **right foreleg** together; his weight levels out as his body stretches more.

■ His head and neck then carry the weight, as they lower to allow **his left foreleg** to touch the ground with ease. On touchdown, the **left foreleg** bears his full weight, together with your weight and that of the saddle and its accompaniments.

■ His back shortens and rounds as both his hind legs are in mid-air coming under his body again.

It is the rocking motion that may make you feel insecure and apprehensive, particularly when the front end of the horse rocks forward as the hindquarters rise; it is at this point when you might bounce up out of the saddle.

You may try to counteract the rocking motion by leaning back when the horse rocks forward onto his leading leg and by tipping forward as the horse's outside hind leg hits the ground.

In effect, rather than working in harmony with the horse, you might attempt to balance yourself by placing your weight opposite to where the horse is placing his.

You must endeavour to sit upright and stay as soft through your body as in the walk.

- Imagine you are a sunflower lifting your face up to the sun; imagine you are sitting in the centre of a seesaw that remains balanced throughout its length.

- Keep your hips separated from your torso. Remember, your pelvis and everything below it belongs to the horse

- Your hips, knees, and ankles must be soft and allowing.

- As you bring your **outside leg** back behind the girth as you ask for canter, your **outside hip** also comes further back than your inside hip.

- Your hips are merely a mirror image of the horse's hips. As he thrusts himself forward with the **outside leg**, his hip on that side also comes back.

Riding turns and circles

The drill of the **traditional aids** and often still seen, is to:

- Ask the horse to bend by putting your **inside leg** on the girth.

- Put your **outside leg** passively behind the girth to prevent the horse from swinging his quarters out.

- The **inside rein** bends the neck.

- The **outside rein** controls the speed and the amount of bend asked for with the inside rein.

Imagine the horse's response when he suddenly feels the crush of a rider's body that is none too sensitive, combined with the rider's confusion and frustration at contending with all the independent movements, even though she may not have the independent seat to facilitate their accuracy and softness.

If your horse shows any signs of discomfort, you may fall into this category. Ideally, you will find a coach who is able to recognise and iron out your issues.

The following **connections** are much easier on the horse and rider, with a more satisfying effect.

The principal connections in the turn are primarily your **outside leg** and the **outside rein.** Combined, they ask the horse to bring his head, outside shoulder and hindquarters over to the inside. At the same time, he is asked to curve his body smoothly around your **inside leg.**

For example, to turn the horse to the left:

- Ask the horse to move off with both of your leg connections.

- Look in the direction of the turn you will ask for – in this case, to the left.

- As you look, the horse will feel the slight movement of your body. He will move in the required direction.

- You simply let your shoulders and hips stay in alignment with the horse's shoulder and hips.

- Place your **outside** (right) leg on the girth area to ask the horse to move into the turn. Your leg encourages the horse to move his shoulder across to the **inside**.

- Simultaneously, the **inside rein** is opened up as you invite him into the space it offers.

- Your **inside** (left) leg shifts slightly back, encouraging him to move around the turn and bend around your leg.

- If your hands are level, you will feel the **outside rein** becoming firmer on the horse's neck as he turns his head and neck to the **inside**.

- If neither hand is in front of the other, both reins will make the same request: the **inside rein** asks the horse to move his head and neck to the **inside**, the **outside rein** gently asks him to move his **outside shoulder** to the **inside**.

- The horse will oblige as he moves away from the gentle pressure of the **outside** (indirect) rein.

- There must be no pulling of the bit on the outside. As his shoulders turn, so will yours.

- **Don't** let your **outside arm** swing forward to ease off the pressure or bring the **outside rein** over the horse's neck. Both will cause him to fall out through his outside shoulder.

- If the **outside** rein is opened away from the neck, the horse will fall **into** the turn of the circle.

- The outside rein defines the size of the circle.

- Your **outside** elbow should remain at your hip while giving the horse a little more rein to allow him to flex his head and neck to the inside.

- **Don't** lean forward because the horse will become heavy through his shoulders and he will be unable to make a correct turn.

- **Always** use your **legs** before your hands. As your **inside leg** and **outside rein** are the main connections for straightness and impulsion, the **inside rein** could be surplus to requirement much of the time.

- Leave the inside rein alone for periods; take notice of how the horse improves!

Experiment with your **outside leg connection** first. If the horse goes around the turn or circle without his legs wandering off their correct tracks, bring in the remaining segments **one**

at a time, perfecting each one until the full connection gently surrounds and cossets the horse as needed.

Omit, then reinstate various connections; feel and see how the omissions and additions affect both you and the horse.

As a reminder, you are working on **perfecting your riding position** so that your connections have natural clarity in the positive influence of the horse. You are **not** simply trying to manoeuvre the horse, as is often the case.

Implant the following phrase into your mind:

> *The inside connections bend the horse;*
> *The outside connections turn the horse.*

The mind is a powerful tool when riding. When sitting correctly and looking in the direction you need to go, all that may be needed is the positive mind video of riding from the inside leg to the outside hand!

A summary

Be as generous to your horse as he is to you.

The tools provided throughout this guide may appear only to slice the tip of the iceberg in their basic form. You may consider some far-fetched. However, be assured that you now own easy to use, valuable and extremely powerful tools.

When used as prescribed, and with the expertise of a coach who can see beyond the '*aids*', you and your horse will advance in all areas, to levels you *never* thought possible before now.

Enjoy your horse; don't take your sessions too seriously.

To concentrate on what you are trying to achieve will hinder your progress.

Play on the swings and roundabouts for a while! Then play a virtual video in your mind of the occurrence required; you will have a much better chance of succeeding.

Show your appreciation of your horse daily. He is *not* here for your exploitation; he is *not* meant to carry you, perform dance movements, or even jump the great heights expected of him. Nevertheless, he does **because he has no choice.**

Be as generous to your horse as he is to you!

Whatever your discipline, keep a constant look out for any negative actions and emotions that your horse may disclose.

Do you truly want to know how your horse is feeling mentally, emotionally and physically? **Then open up your heart and soul to him as he opens himself to you daily. All you need to do then is ask him!**

I am contactable via my email address avis.senior1@gmail.com or my website www.avissenior.com if you have any questions regarding your route to success.'

Recommended

Home Study Theory Based
Certificate Course
www.appliedequinebehaviour.co.uk

Learning theory training principles
and specialist bitless training
Norfolk Horse and Training Club (NHTEC)
Running Free Farm Aylmerton Norfolk

Concordia Equestrians
http://www.concordiaequestrians.com/

Suzanne Rogers BSc(Hons)
Consultant and Behaviourist
Learning About Animals

Printed in Great Britain
by Amazon